To Alif
You have been an inspiration

I And I Are
The Book
I personal self and I Bredren, these are our stories.

enjoy the laugh

Alex Paull

By Alex Paull

Copyright © 2013 by Alex Paull

All rights reserved. Published in the United States by Alex Paull

ISBN: 978-1492154433

*It is that knowledge and wisdom,
far from being one,
have oftentimes no connection, but knowledge dwells in heads
replete with thoughts of other men,
and wisdom in minds attentive to their own.*

James Fenimore Cooper

KNOTTY DREAD AND THE HILLBILLIES

    Sounds of approaching thunder may have brought me closer to waking, but the first sound I actually heard was rainwater rushing into the cistern outside the kitchen door, and when I opened my eyes a rooster crowed. I knew dawn must not be far off. I began hopping up and down on one foot, trying to get my pants on and at the same time move toward the door. No time for shirt or shoes as I ran across the front yard toward the old Dodge truck-- water was forming in pools that splashed as I ran. My feet told me it was going to be close, because by the time water stands in puddles the dirt road leading to Little Indian Creek Farm has already turned to mud. While the truck was cranking, a flash of lightning made the old road shine, and I could see small rivulets of water trying to erode the dirt slowly when the truck fired.
    I revved her hard and slid out onto the road, keeping an even, strong acceleration all the while, trying to get up enough

speed for the first small hill, real wheels fishtailing, spinning the steering wheel sharply in the direction of the slide. I inched up the first hill slowly, and when I reached the top I knew I had a chance to make it, because the final hill had trees overhanging on both sides. Because their branches would keep some of the rain from reaching the road, the clay dirt would still be firm enough to let me get out to the mailbox and the gravel road leading to the blacktop.

 I got out of the truck and headed back to the house. It was a good thing I had my Jamaican walking stick, because when the mud began to squish up between my toes the soft mud on top easily slid against the firmer clay half an inch down, and my bare foot slid toward the shoulder of the road. The walking stick kept me from winding up on my fanny in the mud. No way to start a day.

 It was just now starting to get light. A small pile of sticks clogging the flow of water in the ditch alongside the road caused the water to run out into the middle of the road and erode new ditches that could, in time, make the road even more impassable. I scattered the small blockage with the walking stick and felt only minimally pleased when the water began to cut a channel where it was supposed to.

 "This is it," I thought. "I'm going to talk to Runion tonight because he lived here all his life and he will be able to tell me how to get some stone out of the stingy road commissioner, if anybody can."

 By now I'm fully awake and feel the water running down the back of my neck for the first time. Between tall grasses alongside the road, cobwebs shine silver in the first light. A covey of quail explodes in front of me and half of them sail off into the trees. A few settle in the farmer's field, and I can hear a few running this way and that, out of sight in the underbrush, deciding to make a run for it rather than take off with the group.

 If it is a rainy day in Southern Illinois, the only color you can expect to see in the sky is when the sun first rises red-orange. On closer look, tiny flashes of color shine in drops hanging on invisible webs, like strings of precious stones held together by air and light. I begin to think about coffee, and feeding the chickens, moving the goat and the pony, filling the thermos, eating a little breakfast, and getting lunch together. All of this in time to walk back out to the truck carrying lunch and workboots under my arm in the rain, to try to get into town, to the thirteen-story dormitories at the college, by seven thirty in the morning.

Bright stainless steel elevator doors opened, and I stepped out into the hall filled with hillbilly painters, all dressed in spotless white at twenty to eight, lunch buckets and steaming thermos-tops of coffee by their sides. Although I changed my boots, an obvious smear of mud on the white painters' pants somewhere near the ankle betrays me as a country boy. I was pleased by the simple fact of getting there on time to sit and enjoy a little coffee with the men before eight o'clock.

Since I was a new man on the job, the foreman switches me around with different partners, and although some painters were familiar with my beard, others were from farther out in the country, come in just for this month-long summer job in Carbondale, the largest city around here, to paint the dormitories and to stare at a few young coeds. During the workday we would get to know each other, and the painter would say something like, "You're a nice guy as far as I can see, but why do you want that mess on your face?"

"Because when I used to shave, the places underneath my chin would end up bleeding half the time and it seemed foolish to be sticking these wads of damn tissue paper upside my face to stop the blood from flowing. Some way to start a day."

The issue was dropped. Conversation changed. And in a couple of days I had a different partner, and I could see he was leading up to something when he said, "Could I ask you a question?"

"Sure, ask anything you want," I said.

"Why do you wear that beard?"

"Some of these younger women like the long hair."

The bodies of the coeds were endlessly in the conversations and some men noticed me talking to girls they were too shy to approach. This particular man never said anything more, but in the period of two weeks I also answered playfully to different men, "Some Jamaicans think there is some relation between hair and keeping it up. Or being able to go extra innings if you want."

And then, to another inquiry: "I have to pump the water by hand, heat it up on the wood cook stove. It's too much trouble to shave. Besides, winter is coming and the beard helps keep some of the cold away from my face."

A Rastafarian may read this someday, and he might think, "*Cho!* You appear as a Rastaman and you can't give an *upfull* reasoning about the locks that would be pleasing in the sight of *Jah!*" For this Rastaman's benefit, may I say that there was one Southern Baptist of forty eight years in the painting crew, and he came from a place not on the map called Buffalo Gap, and when he brought up the subject of hair I asked, "Do you read the Bible?"

"You better believe I do!" he said.

"Believe it's true?" I asked.

"God's word," he said, in all seriousness.

"Then look up Leviticus twenty one and Numbers six, and read it for yourself. Everything that is given by God is beautiful and should not be wasted."

The next day Buffalo Gap had done a little reading and while he was cutting in the ceiling above the doors and corners of the room, I was following him, rolling and then cutting in the baseboard. He said, "I looked it up, and it's in the Bible all right. But it also says to let the locks of the hair grow and to separate yourself from other men. Why do you want to do that.

"I don't want to do that," I said. "I never decided to separate myself from anyone. In fact I like to be with different kinds of people. Sometimes you can learn something you don't know, if you pay attention. A couple of years ago I was running a roller rink in Murphysboro, and some of the parents wouldn't let their kids come to the rink. My neighbor, Runion, told me if I got a haircut and shaved off my mustache and change the name of the business, people wouldn't even know it was me. I had this classy California hairstyle back then, and no beard. I got the crew cut and chopped off the mustache to see what would happen. He was right--no one knew me.

"So when this Jamaican herb doctor, Bongo U, asked me if I could put aside the comb, brush, scissors, and razor for a year and see how I felt, it didn't seem like such a big deal then."

"Why do you still keep it?" he asked.

"A year or so went by and then one year I realized that it couldn't be straightened again unless I want a bald-head crew cut. So here I stand, six years later, with a lumpy hat.

"Makes sense," he said tentatively. "At least it stays out of the paint. But how do you get it out of your beard?"

"I don't worry about it, because if I was afraid to get some paint on me I would go pick peaches instead. Besides, if I trimmed it off, my *bredren* in Jamaica wouldn't know me."

"Didn't I hear you say they were supposed to believe in this 'one love' business," said Buffalo Gap. "Then it shouldn't matter to the Rastas whether you cut your hair or not."

"Right," I said, the pace of the roller handle quickening with the excitement of the reasoning. "But there is something else. One day a young Rasta from Kingston who wore long locks was fingering his knife and calling me a *white motherfucking pussyclot* in a not-so-pleasant tone of voice, and an older Rasta says something like, 'Don't he have to bear the same tribulation and reproach as I and I in the eyes of the pagan because him also *dread*?"

"I don't get you," said Buffalo Gap.

"It has something to do with prejudice, I think. Judge a man on his outward appearances only and not by he lives his life, how he treats people."

"Are there a lot of niggers down there in Jamaica?"

"That's all there are down there," I laughed. "But they are more friendly than some American blacks, because they seem to be convinced of their own superiority. At least for making a living in Jamaica where life is really tough, like Depression times must have been around here."

"We could use another good depression," said Buffalo Gap.

"Why do you say that?"

"People are getting too soft. Too lazy. Look at the size and strength of some of these students. And all many of 'em do is lay around after getting drunk half the night."

"Didn't you get drunk when you were a kid?" I asked.

"Sure, but I also worked my tail off to help the family during the hard times. There isn't nothing wrong with these parks we built. Those solid stone walls, wooden bridges and log buildings out at Giant City State Park may be here longer than you and me. Sure, people didn't have much money, but at least they had the satisfaction of earning their own keep."

"You sound like a Democrat, Buffalo," I said.

"It didn't take no Watergate to convince me they're all a bunch of crooks. You could say I'm a Republican, because at least there are fewer of them. There are so many Democrats that you've got to have more crooks too."

"I see," I said, dazzled at his political cynicism. "Rasta calls politrics one word--poli*tricks*."

"That's a good name for it," said Buffalo Gap. "You vote?"

"I almost voted for Kennedy."

"Then you've got no right to criticize what we've got." he said. "I voted for Nixon, so I've got a gripe. I believed in him to the end, a small guy like us, and he made it all the way on his own. Then look what happens. That was the most disappointing thing that ever happened to me.

"I don't know," Buffalo Gap continued. "I may not even vote next time. Maybe I'll just vote local, and to hell with the rest of them. It's about dinner time anyway, ain't it?"

So at lunch this apprentice painter says something to me like, "Hey, Fuzzy, when are you going to get a haircut" in front of all the guys sitting on five-gallon paint cans or on the floor in the dormitory hallway, lunch buckets open, showing canned meat products, sandwiches, Twinkies, cookies, maybe a homegrown tomato, and, of course, coffee and cigarettes. Many showed they were listening carefully looking in their lunch buckets for hidden treasures, or by staring and the smoke rising from their cigarettes. many had asked a similar question, but only in the privacy of a half-painted apartment.

"Do you want to know the truth?" I asked, deciding to play a hand.

"Sure," he said.

"My father is in some banking business in New York, and after i finished college he wanted to set me up. But if he pays for everything I wouldn't feel like an independent man. So I came down here to Southern Illinois and grew this beard, and now he can't find me and give me all this money."

Two guys almost choked on their coffee, one man cleared his throat, and I got a couple of knowing looks from those who may have thought they knew the "real" reason, a couple of murmurs of disbelief, and then the discussion changed as quickly as it began. Over the years, some painter I never saw before would ask me if my father owned a chain of banks in New York, and to this day I'm sure many painters think I am working when I really don't have to.

*****

"This is why now the *Negus* have come and seated up again? Seen? But the first time Him come and Him seated up as the son, now Him seated up as The Father, *the holar* one of creation, is the completion of the trinity. That was the son that seat first, you know, so now when the son come out in a manger, they say, and do all form of miraculous things with Him structure. Seen? And Him now come as The Father."

*****

After work I swung the old truck, fenders splashed with mud from this morning's rain, over to the feed store. I put the roach in the ashtray and went in to pick up a sack of lay mash and a candy bar. Mrs. Dillinger looked up at me, over her glasses. The place smelled of grain dust, processed feeds, and burning creosote in the old stove that John Dillinger kept burning with pieces of railroad ties that he had his student worker help pick up in two-foot sections across the railroad tracks. Even though his business was a success, he still had the Southern Illinois habit of not spending any money. I just had to tease him a little bit.

"John, why do you burn those old railroad ties when you can get lots of hickory and oak from some of these old farmers? The oily smoke is turning your building black, and I just painted it white last year."

"The price is right," was all he said, showing some guy an electric fence snapper.

"Mr. Dillinger," I addressed him good naturedly, "You're too tight for words."

*****

"But now Him come with material power! And all the power then now! Sight!"

*****

When I paid the bill, Mrs. Dillinger's eyes twinkled. She said confidentially, "You know, you would look a lot better if you cut that all off."

"I know I would, Mrs. Dillinger," I said so only she could hear, "but then then the girls would notice me more for sure, and I'm not sure my wife would like that."

She fell into an easy laugh as I tossed the fifty pound sack on my shoulder and headed for the door.

I nosed out into traffic and eased out of town toward the farms and more open spaces. Halfway down the road I passed Karate Joe's place, and I honked and he waved. He was outside messing with his Appaloosas. Karate Joe is this martial arts expert, military in his training, and precise in his obvious dislike for blacks and longhairs. But he was from New Jersey, and us *Joisey boys* seem to be able to stick together.

Crewcut Joe used to keep bothering me about my tam and why I wear a wool hat in August, and I would joke about how the hat kept my head cool--in the sense that I'm sure some would think it uncool to "flash the locks" in view of someone who had never seen it, or never even *heard* of the Jamaican Rastafarians.

One day, Not so long ago, old Karate Joe was bothering me to take off my hat, and so I did, and when the locks came tumbling down over my shoulders like soft coils of brown snakes, he said, "Jesus Christ! Put your hat back on!" He showed in a joking way that in years of asking to see my hair, he did not really want to see it after all. I always wore the bright wool hat to contain the locks, and at the roller rink the kids said, "No hats allowed on the skating floor," so I told him it was part of my belief not to expose my hair in public. The manager later approached me with deep respect in his voice and asked if he could ask a personal question.

"Sure," I said.

"Is it true that it's part of your religion to roller skate with a hat on?"

I drove into the Runion farm still in my white painting clothes, empty thermos beside me on the seat of the truck. I'd come to talk bullshit. I'd finished painting a house for an elder who wanted some organic manure to fertilize his garden the way his father did, and although I didn't need the money that bad, I don't mind handling a little shit now and then if it means something to someone. It's neighborly.

Pappy Runion was up visiting from his retirement in Florida, and was sitting bare-chested and mostly blind in a lawn chair under the shade trees in the front yard. Pete, the rude goose, came up honking and hissing, looking for a chance to grab me behind the back of the leg. He usually lets you pass, and will waddle up unnoticed after the conversation has begun, and nip you, if you aren't careful.

"How you doing, Pappy? What happened, Florida get too hot for you?"

"Just thought I'd like a change." He spat with a precision and neatness off to one side, as if even this unappealing habit could be more acceptable. As if years of practice and listening to a woman complain had taught him well. He had what looked like two week's beard stubble, the hair on his head white and thinning.

"Looks like you got a haircut." I mentioned the obvious, of course, leaving myself open. Although he could barely see, Pappy was certainly aware that over five years had passed without a comb, scissor, brush, or razor touching my head.

"Talking about haircuts, when are you going to get one?"

"I don't know, Pappy. Maybe some woman will come along and spin my head around," I offered.

"Well, more power to her," he said. I thought about Samson and grinned. He did not see me.

"You know me," Pappy said. "I don't give a hoot what anyone says or thinks. I'm nearly eighty years old and I tell it like I see it."

"How do you see?" I asked the blind man.

"I don't care what you do back there in the woods, just so long as I don't have to look at it. If I had to look at it for a half hour, I would be talking to you about getting it cut."

"Appreciate your honesty," I said. "Most people don't say what they feel. They just look away with a *screwface*."

"I say it like I see it."

Finally we got on to the manure and I got the go-ahead to go pick some up over at his barn on Saturday. Pappy's bare feet showed one big toe was missing. Bob Runion came wheelin' in on the 560 tractor, and Pete came waddling out squawking his absurd welcome--or alarm. I couldn't figure out which.

"Well, look who's here. Painting hard?" He saw my whites and the bits of paint on my forearms which I didn't notice at cleanup time on the job.

"Every day," I said. "Some days it seems more work getting out to the hard road than it is painting. I barely made it out this morning."

"I thought you liked it out there in the boondocks where you got to pack a lunch to check the mailbox."

"I do most of the time," I said, "But I don't like to be late for work. I got up when it was still dark, and I just made it by the time I had to walk in, and back out again."

"Leave the truck out at the end of the road when you think it's going to rain. Then you would only have to walk one way," he chided.

"You are a helpful sone of a bitch," I mocked. "But what I need to know is how I can get the road commissioner to get me some gravel. I put that road in practically by myself before the old bridge fell in the creek, and he has been saying since spring he was going to blade it and gravel it. And now fall rains are coming, and I'm still walking in and out in the mud."

"He ain't going to do nothing," Runion said. "Just like the rest of those politicians. The only time they do anything is just before an election, and that's two years from now."

"I can't wait that long. My wife's about to leave me. There must be some other way."

"Well," Runion said slowly, "There is another way."

"I'm waiting," I said.

"They say the wheel that squeaks the loudest gets the grease."

"I'll call that son of a bitch..."

"Now, don't go and make him mad," Bob Runion said gently. "You won't get nothing then but a hard time."

"I've already got a hard time."

When I left Runion's I knew the road would be nearly dry by now, and after checking the mailbox, I carefully drove on the little ridges piled up on either side of the ruts dug by the mudtires at five-thirty that morning. There was still enough moisture to make the mud a kind of claylike consistency that flattened out a little, because water will run down the ruts, making them so deep that the bottom of a regular passenger car would rub on the ground. Just ask Mr. Fenton.

So I called the township road commissioner every other night, and we talked about the weather, the gardens, politics, the shape and condition of township bridges, deer hunting, and any other topic I could think of to keep him on the line as long as possible, to extend the time I kept him away from his television, newspaper, or family. I knew gravel would not be far off.

The roof of the chicken coop was red-lead orange and the old-style fishscale shingles are green with flecks of color, hind which white chickens scratch and peck. I gathered up two dozen eggs, all muddy and nasty-looking because the chickens waded in the mud all day and then walked their muddy feet all over the eggs before they sat down. These birds have got to go, I thought. I don't even eat that many anyway, and it is ridiculous washing these chickenshit eggs for seventy five cents a dozen when I am working every day.

I put the eggs in the kitchen, drank some coffee left over from morning, and took off my work boots, which were turned white from roller spray. I grabbed my machete and basket and headed barefoot for the garden.

Bok choy (called "pop chow" by the Jamaicans) was coming in strong in the garden in front of the barn. I cut off two large green and white heads and put them in the corner of the basket, pulled one yellow and one white onion, and several pods of sweet peas. I shoved the machete tip gently under a dirt hill and popped three red potatoes out of the ground. I walked into the perennial garden and cut some green tops of winter onions, pulled up some garlic, then finished shopping at the herb garden: leaf of sage, a small bunch of thyme, a pinch of oregano, parsley, and chive. If I'd bought a coconut I would have grated it and made soup, but I just washed all the vegetables, cut them up, and started frying first the potatoes and large pieces of Chinese cabbage, added onion and all the rest of the stuff, and had it over rice, seasoned with hot pepper. The *Ital* way. *Ital* means "vital" or natural. No fertilizer, no bug spray--fresh vegetables.

FENTON'S FIELD
1968

If Indian Creek Farm is a wedge of pie, Fenton's field is the crust along which Mottsy and I stretched four strands of barbed wire tight that spring. Both farms are southeast of Boskydell, in the direct path of two hundred hippies who are supposed to be passing our way soon. Mr. Fenton only raises whiteface cattle now, and his field is forty acres of god lespedeza. But he told me he would only plant fescue from now on, because cows will sink into lespedeza and tear it up, while fescue will support the weight of a cow in the soggiest conditions.

The law says neighbors must share the cost of a fence, and seeing as how Mr. Fenton supplied the wire and the posts, Mottsy and I supplied the labor. We were under the careful eye of he who could not do much anymore, coughing gargley deep in his lungs.

"Emphysema," he said, "And do you know I can't just leave these damned things alone, even though they are killing me. Forty years of doing something is a long time."

Mottsy and I rested our arms from pounding the fenceposts in. "Ought to be a law against it," Mr. Fenton said. I wondered if continuous boo smoking would be as bad for me as Camels were for him, but I never said anything to him about it.

The dirt road leading south to Little Indian Creek turns to mud in the rain. It was once a through mail route on horseback, but now it ends fifteen yards past my old oak barn at the newly-stretched fence. Old Man Rushing told me that Fenton had no right to close that road off, and I should tear the fence down. But since there is a culvert washed out halfway down the road to the south, I couldn't see much point to it, except for a shallow kind of vengeance the old man would have against Mr. Fenton.

You see, a few years back a whiteface bull of Fenton's got through the fence and wooed a couple of the old man's black Angus heifers, causing an illegitimate birth which killed her and the calf too, since she was too young to be bred, Old Man Rushing said. Mr. Fenton said that son of a bitch hadn't even offered to share the cost nor the work for either of the fence which he alone stretched between himself and Rushing, and what the hell did he expect putting them heifers up next to the fence all hot and bothered with no Angus bull to take care of them. "No fence would have held him," Fenton said.

What I'm getting at is Mr. Fenton has a sort of illegal fence closing the road (which is actually useless with that culvert washed out), and one time my truck got snowed in at the farm around Christmas time, so I went over to Mr. Fenton's farm to ask if a friend and I might go across his field to try and get my truck out of the mud.

"Come right on in," Mrs. Fenton had said. "We haven't seen you after those beans I gave you, and we was thinking you must have got sick over them and not come back."

"No, nothing like that," I laughed. "They were real good. I've been staying in town part of the time, and been busy the rest."

"Will you take some coffee?" she asked.

"Sure will," I said.

"We stayed up the other night to watch you on the television, and we think you did real good."

"Thank you. I just told why I think the rockfest shouldn't be held around here, that's all. Have you got your tickets for it yet?"

"I don't think we need that kind of thing around here." Mrs. Fenton did not smile at my joke.

"This just ain't no place for it," Mr. Fenton said, "And if it happens, they better not come over on me." He looked toward the fireplace mantel, over which hung a double-barreled shotgun.

"That might do against one or two. Or even ten of them. But it ain't going to stop no mob," I said.

"I got a right to protect what's mine," he said, looking down at the floor.

"I think the court will stop it," I said.

"If it don't, then somebody else will. I'm from the same town as the Shelton boys, and I know the people around here pretty good. Now, it's a long, straight road, that Giant City Blacktop, with hills on either side. One man with a rifle and a scope would be all it'd take, and *that* would be the end of Mr. Harold Calhoun *and* his rockfest. And there wouldn't be too many questions asked, neither."

"I hope the court will stop it," I said.

"Well, it better," he said, coughing low and deep in his lungs. He got up and walked slowly into the bathroom. I heard him spit. Then he came and sat down and finished his Camel. I asked him if I could come across his field to get my truck out, and he said it was all right so long as I didn't make no habit of it, because water will run down where the tire tracks are, and begin to wash out. And he didn't intend to do nothing more with the field because he was getting too old and couldn't do much anymore.

Mottsy and I got the truck started all right, but the snow was slushy and the frost left the ground soft. We needed to tow the truck out with Scout, and that was all right too, except that I complimented the college kid, who was a friend of a friend, on his machine's being able to tow uphill in a slushy field, and he said, "That's nothing--watch this."

Before I could open my mouth, he took off with a roar across the field, cutting the wheels sharp, spinning mud and torn up lespedeza into the air behind, leaving deep ruts in Mr. Fenton's field. The kid was proud of his machine, but I was worried about the field and the fencepost we tore out at the far end where he cut the corner too sharp. I thanked him for helping me get the truck out. When he had gone, I walked slowly into the field, trying to flatten out some of the foot-high ridges in the torn-up pasture by stomping on them, but it wasn't much use. I walked to the farmhouse very slowly, wondering what Mr. Fenton was going to say. He had been watching us through the window all the while.

The old farmer met me at the door, and did not ask me inside this time, so we stood on the back porch. He did not look directly at me either, and when I told him about the fencepost he already knew about, he said there was a pile of posts beside the barn. I went out and put in a new post and told him about the ruts. I asked if I could take a shovel and even them out.

"Mr. Fenton's voice came out dry and flat when he said, "There isn't much you can do with a shovel. I'll go over it with a tractor and disk in the spring."

But I knew he was just saying that. He was getting too old to do much anymore. One thing for sure, he didn't much care even for a lineman crossing his field to fix broken wire, let alone a couple hundred, maybe thousand hippies trying to find a free way into the fourteen-dollar-a-head "Because We Love You" Mayfest of Mr. Calhoun. But what the hell, after forty years of hard work the land was all he owned, and it ain't up to me to say what's right.

BOO!

I took the first drag on the thin cigarette, but it did not draw too well. And when I rolled it between my fingers I felt a fat lump near the unlit end, so I worked it slowly toward the end of the cigarette, and a small round seed jumped out into my open palm.

"Soon it will be time to plant," I said to myself.

This was my third year as farming, but I only counted it as the second, because I lost most of the crop through ignorance. Then I learned how, and in the fall of second year of farming I could not reach the tops of many plants. Even by jumping. Why, the stalks even touched the ceiling of the big walk-in safe of the white-haired sheriff, Ray Dillinger, John's brother, beneath the Jackson County jail over there in Murphysboro.

You see, Old Man Rushing's father, Isaac, who rebuilt what is now my house after a tornado blew it off the hill a few years back, used to pitch manure out the west end of the barn, and that is where the plants grew tallest. I don't mind talking about it some, because by the time you are reading this, Little Indian Creek Farm will be out of the business of boo for good. Or at least until it is legalized.

It was actually that corn-picker neighbor of mine, Bob Runion, and a truckload of hippies who got me started thinking about giving up farming. Bob was about ready to quit farming himself, because there's not much in it anymore. that's probably why he agreed with Mr. Calhoun to park all those cars for the proposed rock-fest on his cow pasture, when he knew all along he was going against almost everybody he knew to do it.

You see, there came a goose-drowner in the early summer of '67 which washed over forty tons of of gravel off Boskydell road and out onto some of the best corn-growing bottom of all in Southern Illinois. Then water covered the ground for several days, which caused large patches of corn to grow up all yellow and stunted. So, after planting and cultivating and worrying after three hundred acres of corn, Bob averaged a little better than a dollar an hour. Why even bother to plant at all? And then, when the promoters told Bob he would get eighty thousand dollars for parking all these rockfest cars on his land at five dollars a car, Bob figured that even if he got a tenth of what he was promised, he would be happy.

I was over at the Runion farm smoking with bob and his housekeeper, who was once his wife. "Now we get along better than ever," Micky said when Bob got up to get some beer. "I know damned well that if this house isn't kept up, all Bob as to say is, "There's the door, honey, and don't let it hit you on the ass on the way out." The television was on, and after we shared the second cigarette, Bob held it before his face and looked at it.

"This must be Boskydell Blue. I've heard it's supposed to be pretty good."

He didn't hear this from me or anyone I know, so I figured my crop must be gaining a reputation of its own, which could be dangerous. I was stuck in town one night and got a ride from a whole panel-truckload of hippies, some I knew, some who knew me, and others I had seen before. We had to go two or three miles out of their way, zigzagging down a chuckhole-filled Boskydell once-gravel road, and so when they led me out I asked the driver if he wanted a little good grass to smoke, and he said, "Fantastic, this is Boskydell Boo, is it?"

My interior caution light was flashing at Runion's, so I kind of mumbled, "I don't know what kind it is. All's I know is that it gets you high." And like I said, one thing an herb farmer does not need is widespread local reputation, except at harvest time.

I told myself that if I could just get away with this one little patch of well-tended boo, I would retire from the farming game for good, just like Bob Runion. But not because there ain't no money in it, that's for sure.

A couple of days later was a cold and rainy night in April, just one month before the giant rockfest would reach Southern Illinois, and lots of farm's ladies around here would donating their fat chickens and making dumplings and cooking big public dinners to raise funds to support their opposition to the festival. Meetings were held regularly, lawyers were hired, and tempers were rising as local farmers like Mr. Fenton worried about their property.

At one of the meetings, a gray-haired man stood up and spoke. "Most of us farmers around here are just normal people who have been here for all of our lives and only want to be left alone. We have lots of neighbors who have known each other a lifetime, and our fathers and grandfathers settled around here a long time back. And now they want to bring all these hippies down here. When I saw for myself on the television, all about that Woodstock business, with open nakedness and drug-taking. All one of our sons or daughters would have to do is go to that rockfest and he could begin taking drugs himself. I've heard they caught some marijuana smokers behind the high school already. We don't need that kind of thing around here at all. Look at what they did in Chicago when they overturned that police car and set fire to it, too. One policeman was killed. And if the police aren't safe, then who is?

He circulated copies of a leaflet among the crowd.

Rock Festival... Good or Bad?

The Rock festival held in Palm Beach County on Thanksgiving Week wound up as completely uncontrolled, filthy in every term of the word, including dirt, obscenities, lewdness, the open use of narcotics and dangerous drugs.

Due to the size of the crowd, officials were incapable of going into the actual amusement compound and merely stayed on the periphery. Regardless, there were approximately 122 persons arrested for marijuana, narcotics and dangerous drugs. Outside toilets were frequently not used except by patrons who locked themselves in, in order to shoot heroin. Many of the participants urinated openly. Garbage, trash and debris of all kinds filled the area, mixed with mud, beer cans, bottles, clothing, blankets etc. scattered around. Lewdness and obscene conduct and sexual acts were not uncommon.

The Intelligence Unit of the Palm Beach Sheriff's Office has advised that the scene left by the festival was unbelievable--the filth, trash, garbage, etc. They advised that most of the persons who had been arrested had ten dollars or less on their person and that another large percentage had less than five dollars.
Presented as a Public Service by the
DOWNTOWN KIWANIS CLUB, 704 INGRAHAM BLVD.
(Taken from the Miami Herald, Miami Florida.)

After the meeting was over and I had a stomach full of chicken and dumplings, I went over to Runion's farm. I knocked and opened the back door. No one ever uses the front door because it is blocked off by a huge freezer that holds garden vegetables and a venison Bob short last fall in the fencerow between his corn and the creek. The deer eats Bob's corn, then Bob eats the deer.
"Hello," I said, loud enough for him to hear me above the sound of the TV and barking dogs.
"Well, come on in," he hollered over the racket.
Half a dozen little runt dogs swirled around my feet, jumping and yapping, and I followed the sound of the television into the front room where Jack and Bob were sitting. After a big meal, Bob sat in the green recliner with his shoes off, leaning back. On the couch along the south wall sat Jack, Bob's friend from upstate. They both looked bearded and scruffy and tired and full.
"Go fishing today?" I asked.
"Ever-day," Bob said.
"I don't see how you can fish everyday," I said. It seems like if you lay off a day or two you might enjoy it more."
"Easy," he said. "All I have to do is think about work and I just go right on fishing." He made a casting motion with his right arm. The three of us laughed, but we all knew that when the

ground is dry enough Bob Runion will work seven days a week, from around eight in the morning until dusk. A total of around eighty-four hours average, with an occasional rainy day to work in the shop on tractor and machinery repairs.

"But even that night work," I said. "I don't see how you can hit for half an hour every night like you say you do." I winked at Jack.

"If you like something, you do it every day. Or else you really don't like it as much as you think you do."

"Everything gets old after awhile," Jack said with a sigh.

I went into the kitchen and brought back three beers. When I sat down the color TV news was turned low, flashing pictures of an American tank firing machine gun bullets into the jungles of Cambodia before smashing its way through the underbrush. When the tank came into a clearing I could see a large white peace symbol and an herb leave crudely painted on its steel sides. "Here you go," I said, putting down the beers.

Whatdehellugodowarove?

"I got my truck stuck up again yesterday," I said. "And when my boss Woody came out to help me, he got his new truck with the positraction stuck up to the axles too. And it took us three hours to get both trucks out of the mud. It was a good thing we had a little Black Jack Daniels whisky to smooth over the work. We hardly knew we was in the mud."

"Don't you know enough yet to stay off that dirt road after it rains? It ain't never going to hold you up," Bob said.

"Then how the hell is your pasture going to hold up all those rockfest cars next month?" I asked.

"Might not rain 'til I get them on there," Bob said. "Then they'll pay me to get them off."

"Farmer's Almanac says rain," I said.

"Can't believe all you read," Bob said.

"Well if it *does* rain, how are you going to get them out of there?"

"I ain't worrying about getting them *off* my land. Just so's I get them *on* there at five dollars a car. Besides, the promoters say they will bring in steamrollers and pack the ground so it will hold up the cars."

"Do you think it will work?" Jack asked.

"Won't know until we try," Bob said.

"You still think they are going to have it?" I asked.

"Sure do," Bob said. "They are out there right now building the crappers."

"How many do they have done?"

"About twenty six eight-holers."

"That leaves over four hundred to go," I said.

"They are working on them twenty four hours a day."

"They haven't even got the water for it yet."

"They got tanks in St. Louis all ready to be brought in, and permission from the mayor to buy and haul city water out to the site. They're going to have it."

"Bet you five they're not."

"You're on," Bob said, sitting forward in his chair. I got up from the sofa and shook his hand.

"Hell, there's only three weeks left in April. The judge will stop it."

"Dammit, you can't stop a man from doing what he wants with his own land, so long as he doesn't break no laws doing it. Well, people should be able to drive down the damn road, and with all those thousands of rockfest cars--"

"Now what are you talking about? You can only drive down *your* road if it don't rain!" he laughed.

"I got to agree with you there," I said, laughing after him. "Just have your five ready after the eleventh of next month."

"Don't think I'll need to."

"Well, I got to be getting back." I said.

"No need to rush off," Bob said.

"Got to go," I said. I closed the back door behind me because, like I said, there is no way to enter or leave the Runion farmhouse from the front.

When I got back to Little Indian Creek Farm, I took out the *Old Farmer's Almanac*. I was actually bluffing Bob a little bit, and I wanted to see if it was really going to rain on the rockfest weekend. Early May, 1970. As if you could tell by the book.

On page thirty one, it said:

Weather

I sigh,
I cry
a
wicked storm
is nigh.
No
cheer
here
dear.

Grass is green,
may-
flowers blush
un-
seen.
Rains
terrible
in St.
Louie
and D.C.
Eggs
forsooth
will fry
on
the roof.

(The 1970 <u>Old Farmer's Almanac,</u> Robert T. Tomas, Yankee, Inc.)

ACCORDING TO PERCY THE BAKER:

May the words of my lips and the meditation of my heart
    be acceptable in Thy sight, oh Jah,
      my strenght and my redeemer who liveth
      and reigneth over all human etherience.

BOSKYDELL

Southern Illinois is a quiet corner of the universe, often hiding in little fern-covered hollows between gently rolling hills, towering cliffs of sandstone, between the mighty Mississippi and the Ohio rivers, more south than most of Kentucky. Changes happen slowly around here, a reason, maybe, why many of us have grown to love these back roads full of potholes and washboard surfaces with lots of spaces between the houses, woods of tall white oak and hickory, gardens and orchards of red apples and orange peaches to please the eye.

When the Illinois Central Railroad was built in the early 1800's, a large quantity of stone was needed for culverts and ballast. This stone was quarried from the sandstone bluffs surrounding Boskydell. When the state of Illinois was building a teacher's college at Carbondale, the red sandstone was taken from the Boskydell quarry. After the "Old Main" building was finished, stone was shipped to the state capitol at Springfield.

A report written in 1882 suggests that Boskydell is not likely ever to be much of a town. It had already gained a reputation for rowdyism. Murders happened there.

More houses were needed in Boskydell. E.M. Hanson laid out an addition to the town in 1877 and several more houses were built. The town is in the valley of Drury, six miles to the south of Carbondale. The reason I bring up this short history is that Boskydell is close to the heart of the country. A few miles south of the actual geographical heart perhaps, but nonetheless the heart by the intensity of feelings surrounding it.

Back around 1850 men were taking the red sandstone from Boskydell, loading it onto wooden wagons pulled by mules into Carbondale, and building the foundation and much of the hand-cut stone decoration for the "Old Main" building, the first building of any size or importance on the campus of Southern Illinois University. At that time, when the first story had been built and the workmen were hoisting joists in the center of the building, the joists fell on the builder, J.M. Campbell, and killed him. This put a temporary stop to the construction.

Over a hundred years later that grand building was destroyed by a fire set by radicals. I guess they were trying to say something about the future, or maybe about the past. You can't buy sandstone like that today. It was cut out by hand from the rock ledges around Boskydell, and Boskydell is no longer even a town.

Around the time of the Great Depression and for twenty years thereafter there was a red and yellow railroad station in Boskydell where you could buy a ticket north to Chicago or south to Memphis. The station was used mainly to ship asparagus and peaches and apples to Chicago. There was a station house with a waiting room and a potbellied stove. Men used to sit around the station in bad weather, or after sending their crops to market. They'd talk about farming or about horses, or maybe hunting dogs.

A man who knew something about Boskydell was old John Crowell. He was a retired barber in Carbondale. For over forty years he cut hair, after farming for twenty. When he was seventy his wife died, leaving him alone. He had used to tremble a little when he cut my hair on his back porch. I used to be fussy about my hair before I met John, but he didn't have much to do anymore and he did the best he could. That was good enough for me.

John held up the mirror. "It looks fine, Uncle John," I said. "How much do I owe you?"

"You don't owe me nothing at all. I've got little use for money anymore."

Sometimes I brought some friends over with some red wine, and John Crowell used to quote the Bible a lot. He once said, before taking the first glass of wine from my hand, "Jesus didn't have nothing against wine. He made some of the best wine ever tasted on this earth. He thought so much of it He used it as His blood in the Holy Sacrament. Wine is given as a natural comfort to man, so long as he doesn't misuse the privilege and make himself uncomfortable by it."

We gave what would be the last birthday party for Uncle John, and we fixed a big chicken dinner with dumplings, wine, smiles, handshaking, and general congrats at his reaching eighty two. John said how it did his heart good to be around young people, and how in them lies the strength of the future.

It took a lot of coaxing, but one summer day John finally got into the old truck with us and took a ride into the country. We drove through Boskydell and he showed me where the boardwalk used to run from the train station to the church. We came down the dirt road, bounced up the few ruts, and stopped in the shade of the maple trees in the front yard. John said he used to hunt rabbits all around Fenton's field, and he said he never thought he would get to see this part of the country again.

When we got back to town Uncle John was tired. We stood on the back porch and he told me he used to shoot marbles when he was a kid back in Boskydell. He gave me a whole fruit jar of handmade marbles he had won, most of them not quite round, the colors of the earth. Clays of brown, soft gold, and yellow, but a few of the marbles were colored soft green and red, and just one had three pale blue lines on it, fading, rich as the sky, worn smooth by many children's hands for nearly a century.

There are only two theories about the training of a horse. The first says that when you are in the saddle and your horse rears up, simply bring a two-by-four down with all your might between his ears, and if he rears again, swing down with both hands this time and bring him to his knees. The theory is that the horse will not rear up a third time because by now he is convinced that if he does come up again, there will be a big stick waiting to clunk him on the head. And indeed there is.

The second theory of learning suggests that when your horse rears and jumps around he is simply nervous or hyperactive, so get down from the saddle, walk around front, reach in your pocket and give him a bite of grain, talking gently and stroking him all the while so that he relaxes and eventually becomes your friend. If you give the horse half a chance he will recognize you and carry you all over the countryside, thinking dully of the barn and of sweet lespedeza.

There are as many variations of these two theories of learning as there are ways of looking at God, and what He is or isn't going to do for us. As far as I could see, however, there were only two theories of compulsory education--the axehandle overhead method , and the grain before the nose bethod. CDF and AB, in academic terms.

Speaking of compulsory education--up at "The Normal School," which is what they once called Southern Illinois University, Dr. William A. George met Bill George, the Anteater. The first William George was a doctor of zoology, and he wore a neat gold tweed suit with a wide tie hanging at his neck. He was about to lecture with a slight lisp on the topic "The Extinction of Bird Species Throughout the World, and Its Relation to Ecology,' when Bill George chained his chopper to a steel post holding up a limp flag right in front of the building. He wore a Levi's jacket with the sleeves cut off, open in front to a white tee shirt molded around his large belly. His black boots were big, and so was his bent nose, resulting in the nickname "Anteater."

Earlier that day Anteater was rearing up and down the streets of collegetown on his Harley when someone handed him this flyer about how he was going to lecture that evening on birds, so he thought he might just ride over to the campus and meet his other self. The lecture was almost over when he clomped down the center aisle and sat down in the middle, three rows from the front. The audience is mostly of a conservative, bird-watching variety, and Anteater sat down with a headful of wild hair, and who knew what else.

Dr. William George lost his place for a moment, but quickly recovered himself, cleared his throat, and went on about the protection of the ruby-throated honey-sucker in East Africa. This little bird has a mysterious bond with several tribes of men. When a man wants to find honey, he listens for the call of this bird and then the bird leads the man to the bees' nest. When the honey is drawn from the hollow tree, the man leaves some beeswax to one side for the ruby-throated honey-sucker, who then uses it for nesting purposes. If someone should kill one of these birds, his ears are cut off. Hearing this last bit of information, the audience laughed.

Dr. George went on about how there are virtually no federal laws protecting many birds from extinction in America, which has resulted in the total destruction of the prairie chicken, the passenger pigeon, and several others. And how the vicious capitalist system has leveled off vast areas of swamp in Florida, which is the nesting area of the swamp warbler, and how the entire species is on the verge of extinction. Anteater stood up and said, "We all know there's problems, but do you have any answers?"

The birdwatchers shifted in their seats. The professor unbuttoned his gold tweed coat. "No," he said. "Any answer would involve the changing of the system, which is too large and complex to--"

"Then you're just copping out!" Anteater shouted up at him.

The good doctor shouted back, pointing a stiff finger from the podium. "You're just bullshitting! What good have you done! You haven't done anything either, and you've got no right--"

"You're the one that's bullshitting! Birds are one thing, man, and if you ain't done nothing to help them out, you got no right standing up there and telling us about how bad things are. It ain't what you talk about. It's what you do!"

The doctor looked for a moment as though he might explode all over the auditorium. Then his voice came out strained, as if some kind of pressure was forcing his words. "I did do something," he said. "There was a company right here in Illinois which was dumping waste into a marsh area which endangered a certain species of swamp duck. I found out the company was underpaying its men so I met with them and forced them to dump elsewhere."

The birdwatchers clapped and hooted and the doctor was openly astonished at the applause. He blushed a little at all the attention, but everyone was behind him now. As the applause faded, Anteater, still standing, said, "Now wait a minute here. The point is that you weren't gonna say nothing about what you and me can do to help some of the problems in America. That ain't right. If you have any answers, what are you hiding them for?"

The applause had calmed William George some, and without raising his voice he said to Bill, "You are correct about that. I would not have mentioned it had I not become angry, because, after all, blackmail is against the law, you know."

Anteater walked up to Dr. William George and said loud enough so we could all hear, "I'm glad to know someone who actually did something to help, and I want to shake your hand. If you're ever down at PK's I'll buy you a beer."

Anteater clomped out of the auditorium through the applause to his chained chopper. He released the bike from the flagpole, kicked it until it roared, and then rode away from the university to get some beer. His heart was still beating fast. maybe he wasn't used to teaching.

A week later, Kent State exploded all over the media. Then on May 8, 1970, two thousand, five hundred young people moved down the main street, University Avenue, with Anteater on his Harley at the lead, a wide grin beneath his hooked nose. He could tell it was party time.

Anteater was a local good old boy whose mother owned a small house just north of where the First National Bank now stands. Back in the late 60's there was an old hospital on the bank site and over two thousand people moved past the grass and trees that were once bright green, where there is now a parking lot south of the Dairy Queen. No one really knew what they were going to do on May 8, and there were no famous speakers or charismatic leaders to inspire us, because old Anteater was only looking for a good time.

The long lines of young people finally stopped at the intersection of Route 13 and University Avenue, filling the old train depot parking lot, where the group had permission to hold a rally. The center strip was closed but Highway 13 remained open. Everyone sat down in the main crossroads of Carbondale for about three hours. Many were there just to party. Some got drunk, others got stoned. And some were talking about what should be done to stop the war in Vietnam.

No words of wisdom were coming over the microphone, but a young woman said, "We are going to stay here peacefully and make our opinions known." The Illinois State Police routed the traffic around the intersection and many kids talked of staying all night. It was a warm spring night and the group recited the Pledge of Allegiance, and drank, and sang the opening lines of "The Star Spangled Banner." I felt very patriotic.

Old Anteater came up to the microphone. He was one of the first born-again Christians, in his spare time, and he began to recite the 23rd Psalm:

"The Lord is my shepherd. I shall not want. He maketh me to lie down. In green pastures. He leadeth me--"

"Oh, wow, man, a religious freak!" someone from the crowd shouted up at the speakers stand.

"Let him finish," someone else shouted.

"Shut up, it ain't Sunday!"

"Yea," Anteater chanted, "though I walk through the valley of death I will fear no evil. For thou art with me--"

And then no more than twenty-five people stood up, went over, and sat down on the railroad tracks of the "Mainline of America," as the Illinois Central Railroad proudly called itself, and blocked the Panama Limited needed north to Chicago.

Anteater was now trying to remember all the words to the Lord's Prayer and was arguing over the microphone with some woman about what phrase came next. Some of Anteater's audience rose to their feet and tried to talk the two dozen people into getting off the tracks, because, after all, they had been "allowed" to occupy the intersection by the police. The smaller group took a vote and decided to continue holding up the thirty thousand tons of iron from moving the U.S. mail on schedule.

A young woman grabbed the mic from Anteater and said, "Hundreds of Americans are dying every week *for nothing*, and all some people can think about is their damned schedules! It's about time people stopped what they are doing and think about what their country is doing!"

She got applause from the two dozen track sitters, while the larger group still tried to convince the smaller group to get off the tracks. Meanwhile, back at some strategic command headquarters, a meeting was being held among the Carbondale Police, the Illinois State Police, the Jackson County Sheriff's office, the SIU Police, and the Illinois National Guard.

Their decision was to disperse the demonstrators from the intersection and from the railroad tracks. Gas, rather than riot batons or other means, was to be used. Green army jeeps with rolls of barbed wire on their front bumpers rolled on back streets. The state police moved up near the crowd, sledge hammer handles up front. Two city policemen fired tear gas over the heads of the Panama blockers into the larger crowd sitting peacefully in the intersection. Then state police fired more gas into the crowd and the National Guard moved in, shoulder to shoulder with gas masks, to back up the state men.

The gas fell, then rocks and wine bottles flew, and everyone ran, crying, down back alleys, looking for somewhere to release the tensions and frustration of being gassed for what someone else did. Did they really expect the students to return quietly to their dorms? Over a hundred businesses were left with broken windows. Then came the civil emergency, the clubbing, the arresting, and the 7:30 curfew.

Two days later the curfew was lifted and some dormies drifted outside Brush Towers, the biggest skyscraper in Southern Illinois. Looking to take in some night air, maybe. The police ordered them to move, citing a local ordinance. When the police insisted in a threatening stream of four-letter words, several kids tossed rocks at police cars as they ran. Maybe some of the rock throwers were yesterday's gas-smellers, I don't know. But they ran inside Stevenson Arms dorm and the entire building, housing a couple dozen men, was gassed. The smoke forced everyone out into the streets, crying and coughing. The curfew was promptly re-invoked, and everyone was forced back inside the gassed building. There were a lot of dormies and Greeks and beer-drinkers as well as peace freaks mad that week.

In dormitories a thousand people live close together. In stevenson Arms everyone's clothes and rooms reeked of gas, and each had his own story to tell. The news moved fast and lots of kids rode on the excitement, with thousands cheering outside the window. "It's your school, too! Join us! Join us!"

When the smoke finally cleared on the 13th of May, the university closed, in broken glass. Three thousand students demonstrated to keep the college open, five thousand demonstrated to close it. After a very dramatic and democratic vote called by the university president, Delyte Morris, the headlines of the *Daily Egyptian* college paper read "SIU Closed Indefinitely."

That night University Avenue in Carbondale witnessed five thousand people partying in the street with firecrackers to keep the cops nervous, and helping celebrate the fact that school was out for the summer. They went on all night until daylight with beer and wine, pot, and who knows what else. There was little broken property. The police had orders to stay out of the way this time and there was no gas.

The party was still going on in the street at three in the morning when Woody, my painting foreman, was driving back to his motel after helping close half the bars in the county. His truck found itself right in the middle of the student crowd.

"I kept the doors locked and windows rolled up," he said later, "and kept the air conditioner on. One of them even climbed up the hood of my truck, walked up over the windshield, up the top of the camper, and on down the other side. And I didn't say nothing. There were cases of beer and bottles of wine all over the place, and some of them were sitting at the edge of the street like a bunch of Indians. I even saw somebody pissing on the street! But I have to say one thing for them. They had litter barrels and were picking up the beer cans and the wine bottles right behind them as they went."

While I was working next to Woody the next day I tried to explain that out of those four hundred people arrested earlier, some had thrown rocks and some hadn't, and some just happened to be in the way of the violence and were clubbed down with axe handles and arrested, to find themselves shaken entirely out of their complacency and their apathy.

"Well, Goddammit," Woody said. "If they'd all stayed over in their dormitories where they belonged, the police could catch the instigators and the agitators and lock them up. They got no business in the street, and if they busted a few more heads like they did that first night and had a mandatory one year in jail for every one of them caught rioting, maybe there will be an end to all this shit. They're turning them loose as fast as they catch them, and what do they do. They go right on back to rioting."

I argued with Woody. "I know a sixteen-year-old kid who lives near the campus and he went up to see what was going on. He was standing near the iron fence in front of Old Main building, watching, when everybody started running around him. He stood still because he wasn't doing anything wrong, so why should he run? A university policeman about twenty-one years old clubbed him in the head. Bobby fell to his knees, and when he tried to get up, he was smashed across the shoulders. He crouched like an animal, crying 'What do you want me to do? What do you want me to do?' And he was dragged off toward the police car. 'Do you need any help?' another policeman asked. 'No, this one's mine,' he said. 'I got this one.'"

Woody said, "I still say if he's stayed home where he belonged he wouldn't have got in no trouble. If everybody would just stay home where they belong, the police could find the rock throwers. But no, everybody's got to stand around and see what's going to happen. If I was that kid's father, after I paid his bail, I would have kicked his ass all the way back home. The next time he would stay where he belonged."

Woody was a painting foreman in St. Louis, fifty-two years old. I tried to tell him that, sure, if everybody stayed home there would be no problem, but people aren't staying where they belong anymore. Woody still believed that if everybody would just stay home the problem would go away. And Woody was right. One thing for sure, though--the kids aren't afraid. I asked that sixteen-year old high school junior Bobby Russell after all that happened, would he go to another rally? "Yeah," he said, "I'd go again. But next time I'm going to bring something with me."

"A rock?" I asked.

"No. No rocks for me. I'm going to get some of that spray stuff."

"You can't just go out and buy Mace."

"Maybe not exactly mace, but something just like it. They sell it in drugstores for ladies to put in their purses. It's called "Mug Arrester," and it's as big as a fat pen. The next time somebody tries to beat me for nothing, I'll go down like this."

Bobby raised his arms as if to ward off a blow and he dodged to the side like in the western movies, drawing from his pocket at the same time the can spraying upward and under an imaginary plastic face mask as he hit the ground.

"Somebody better get a hold of this before it's too late," Woody said. "The merchants will be ready for them next time. The insurance doesn't cover all this damage, and many of them are standing watch in their stores with guns. The next time somebody is going to get a belly full of hot lead, and then maybe that will stop some of this shit."

  Consider that we in Boskydell live on a major earthquake fault, the New Madrid. It's not surprising then, that even quiet corners of the universe sometimes shake and tremble when major issues surface. Some say the riots helped end the war, and others are convinced that the days of anarchy were Carbondale's darkest hours. Anyhow, if you refuse to leave some beeswax for the ruby-throated honey-sucker, or refuse to appreciate and respect the innocence of a young Bobby Russell, you better hold on to your ears.

WHOM DO YOU REPRESENT?

"Somebody's got to do something," I thought bravely, standing in the phone booth at the old Carbondale bowling alley, out by Murdale, on my lunch hour, in coveralls all spotted brown with speckled wood stain thrown from the spinning roller cover.

So I called up the lieutenant governor, Paul Simon, in Springfield. The first secretary said I couldn't talk to Mr. Simon right then because he was addressing a house. When I asked her for an appointment, she said that Mr. So-and-so handles the scheduling of appointments. Then she asked me, "What group of citizens do you represent, Mr. Paull?"

I could see the waitress bring the food. Woody, my foreman, was looking over at me from the table, and I ad-libbed quickly. "The Concerned Citizens of Southern Illinois."

"Are you the president of that group?"

"No," I said, thinking fast. "I am a spokesperson for the group." There was a pause, as if she was writing.

"And what is the nature of business you would like to discuss with the lieutenant governor?"

I kind of stumbled around for awhile because I hadn't gotten my story quite together yet. I mumbled something about how people were completely polarized around here, and were arming themselves against each other. My group, I said, had come up with some alternatives to to violence.

The first secretary said, "I will let you talk with Mr. So-and-so, who handles the appointments. He is not here right now, but he should be in by two o'clock. Is there a number where I can reach you?"

Most of lunch break was over by now, and there are no phones back at the job. "No, there is no number where I can be reached. I will try and call back at two."

At two, I took my last break and called up Springfield. I asked for Mr. So-and-so. The second secretary said, "Mr. Simon is out of the Assembly meeting, and Mr. So-and-so has gone out for something to eat. Can I have him return your call? What is your name, please, and the nature of your business?"

I told her.

"What group do you represent?"

"Don't you already have that information? I'm the same man who called earlier."

"No," she said. "That was Mary Ann you talked with this morning. I am filling in while she is on her break. Can I have her call you?"

"No, there is no phone where I work." I raised the receiver as if to bap the machine upside the head with its own plastic arm, and then I got lucky.

"Here comes Mary Ann now. She will talk to you."

"Hello, Mr. Paull. Yes, I remember you. Mr. Simon is still in conference and won't be in his office until two-thirty."

"The other secretary said he was out to eat," I said, cold as a stone in the snow.

"Oh, yes. That's right. I just now got back in the office myself. I'm sorry for the inconvenience, sir. If there was just some number where you can be reached--"

"Well, there isn't. I'll try again later. Goodbye."

Then Bell Tel ate up two more dollars and I felt bad about being rude, but I believed I was getting closer. Over five dollars gone, though, as well as my last coffee break of the day. And Mr. Simon might be out of his office by the time I got off work.

I left the job like I was going to the crapper, and I sneaked over to the phone, looking for Woody to catch me taking and unauthorized break. Union work is kind of strict that way. I invested three more quarters, and I heard a familiar female voice.

"Hello, Mary Ann? This is Mr. Paull again."

"Oh, yes, Mr. Paull. Mr. Simon's assistant will receive your call now. One minute, and I will connect you."

"Yes, Mr. Paull. Can I help you?" Mr. So-and-so's voice was deep and respectable.

"I would like to make an appointment with Lieutenant Governor Simon."

"Yes, I will see what I can do for you, but first let me ask you a few questions. What group or groups do you represent?"

"I am a spokesperson for The Concerned Citizens, sir."

"Do you represent just one county?"

"No," I lied. "Several counties--Jackson, Williamson, and Union."

"The lieutenant governor is already informed about the rockfest and the closing of the college."

"This isn't only about the rockfest. My group got together and decided that something has to be done about what is happening in Southern Illinois before there is some big trouble. We have some very definite suggestions that we think he should be personally aware of."

"I understand, Mr. Paull. The House is meeting now and we are all very busy around here."

"I see," I said stiffly.

Mr. So-and-so found a small ray of hope. "We will fit you in before or after the meeting on Thursday But it is impossible to arrange a definite appointment for you. If you call our office when you arrive in Springfield some time between nine and ten, we will try and have a more definite answer for you by then. You may have to wait until the afternoon to speak with Mr. Simon. If we can't fit you in the morning."

"That will be fine," I said. "I know you are very busy up there. You will hear from me when I get to the capital. Don't call me, I'll call you. Should I call you personally, sir?"

"No. Please call the original number."

"Oh, you mean Mary Ann?"

He paused. "Yes, that's right."

I sneaked back to the job and Woody hadn't missed me. He was shellacking the penthouse doors at Carbondale Memorial Hospital. I went back to staining as fast as I could. After a few minutes I said to Woody, "I don't like the way things are being run around here. I think I'll go talk to the lieutenant governor and get things straightened out."

"That's a damned good idea," Woody agreed. "They ought to bust a few more heads around here before it is too late. The shopkeepers are not going to stand for any more broken windows." Woody moved the roller, spreading shellac smoothly up the doors I had stained yesterday.

"You really believe I'm going to see the lieutenant governor?"

"If you say so. I always believe what someone says until I learn otherwise. It might do some good. What are you going to tell him?"

"I'm not sure yet. I'm still thinking about it. But at least I got an appointment to talk with him. I heard he's a smart man and a competent leader." I pushed back my red and white polka-dot sly hat. It was like a hat worn by Uncle Briggs, the guy who hosted the afternoon cartoons.

"Wish you luck," Woody said.

"Thanks," I rolled dark brown stain up wooden doors for the rest of the afternoon. I thought about what I would say to Paul Simon next Thursday that might help keep some of the stone throwers and the stick thumpers from tearing each other up.

I had the weekend to think of what to say to the politician. By Saturday I was still lost. I was driving down Boskydell Road and passed the place where the old sawmill once stood, near the wooden boardwalk where Old John Crowell had won his driveway. I pulled into Michael Ontken's driveway. He was a teacher in the SIU art department.

Michael had just finished a vegetarian meal. He sat watching television. Like me, he had found himself living near Boskydell with a small garden to work in.

"Come on in," Michael said. I sat down on a round stool made of ancient white oak. Highly detailed color drawings filled almost every wall. On a table made from a door was a sketch of an old king lying on his back on a wooden stretcher held several inches off the ground by forked sticks. The king looked stone-stiff, and you could just barely make him out, the grass grew so thick around him. Weeds grew up through his hair and flowing white beard. It looked like he had been there a long time. The king's body was not decayed, but from out of the matting of his beard and from between the chinks of his armor worms moved and turned into butterflies near a chalice that stood at his feet. The butterflies flew off toward a rising sun in irregular patterns.

"What have you been up to?" Michael Onken asked.

"I'm going to see the lieutenant governor next week."

"What about?"

I decided to state the obvious. "Something has got to be done or somebody is going to get hurt bad around here."

"Right. So what can you do?"

"This whole damn eruption started at the confrontation at the railroad tracks. There were fifteen hundred people sitting in the center of town, drinking wine and smoking grass, and talking of alternatives to violence while surrounded by all the opposing forces. And so the police routed traffic around all this mess. And then twenty-five people go and sit on the tracks. If I had been in charge that night, I sure would have not shot tear gas into the middle of that crowd and scattered them all over town pissed as hell. There had to be some other way to get those few people off the tracks."

"So you think maybe some of the police wanted to knock a hairy head with an ax handle? And would have found a reason to, eventually? Very few people at such times can feel any respect for anyone who is not on the same side. That goes for both sides."

"But as soon as you have two large groups of people pushing near one another, the extremists on both sides will start pushing for action," I said. "What if there could be a few people who would be somewhere between the lines so that the extremists on both sides would be calmed? So that one group wouldn't attack the other? Do you know anything about the Hog Farmers? I heard that the Woodstock people flew some Hog Farmers all the way up to New York in a specially chartered plane. They are supposed to be so psychologically aware that they can see where most people are coming from. They can relate to them in a way that brings understanding and peace, calming them with reason and affection. Some might say love. Maybe they're leftover Beatniks or something.

"I heard that at Woodstock there was a crisis involving lots of people with rising tempers," I continued. "And after several attempts to reach out with reason failed, one of the Hog Farm chicks took off her clothes and started giving away flowers and joints and everybody started laughing and forgot what they were mad about. What I'm getting at, Mike, is if some of these kinds of people were trained in what has worked in other confrontations, maybe they would know how to get the twenty-five people off the tracks so that the larger group wouldn't be gassed." It seemed reasonable to me.

"Now, how many people do you know who would want to be paid by the state to be in a special task force? Then you would be considered a counter-revolutionary by some people, and that could get dangerous. And I'm not so convinced that anything can or should be stopped. I doubt if you could find anyone heavy enough to handle the job, and if you could, I doubt that he would want to do it.

"Besides," Michael added, "We tried your idea in a way and it didn't work. That's why I feel the way I do now."

"Who tried it?" I asked.

"Me and some people from the art department. And one guy from English. Tom and Lowell Darling both tried talking to the demonstrators, and Lowell got hit by a cop who thought he was a leader of the group. Lowell had grabbed the mike to try and calm people down. And when Tom tried to talk to them, they yanked the mike away from him before he had a chance to say anything.

"I'm not sure we should try and stop it," Michael went on. "Even if there was a chance we could. Besides, the riot was probably the most exciting thing that has ever happened in some of those kids' lives. Just to be a part of something real. To actually make a small part of history. I saw one freshman girl with a round, sweet face saying, "Right arm, right arm," and giving the Panther salute. She didn't know what was happening, but she was in there just the same."

"What about all the heads busted in?" I asked. "All the damage. The escalating violence."

"I know what you mean, but maybe it's got to happen that way. The extremists on both sides have to go before we can have any kind of harmony. How can you have a workable system including a lot of people who believe that another group of people should not even be allowed to exist? You would have the same thing all over again, and the winners will be those not involved. Hopefully."

I couldn't come up with anything to say just then, which is rare for me. I usually have a mouthful of words, as you can tell by this book.

"And for now we can dull the senses," Michael said, and we did, and watched images change across the screen until the moon moved far into the west. When I finally drove back to the farm there was a small, bright light in the eastern sky. I've been told that the Indians believe that if you are awake in time to see the morning star, it will bring good fortune.

On the day before my appointment with the government official, I asked Woody for the day off.

"You really believe I'm going to talk to the lieutenant governor?"

"I believe anything someone tells me until I catch them in a lie once," said Woody.

"But it'll cost me fifty bucks in wages, and I already spent over five in phone calls just to get the appointment. And I don't have any license plates on a truck with bald tires. What will I tell the cop that stops me? 'You can't stop me! I have an appointment with the lieutenant governor!"

Woody laughed and said maybe I could borrow a car. Or maybe someone would want to go with me. "Maybe I'll call the capital," I said, "and have him send down a state limo for me. But I still have to borrow a suit. Do you think I should wear a tie?"

"*Bow*tie," Woody said, not smiling.

"He'll think I'm a waiter."

Woody and I both laughed at that, but I later found out that Paul Simon wears a bowtie himself. He wrote a book about how Catholics and Protestants can make a marriage work. I was beginning to think more and more that I did not have anything to say tomorrow. I went over to Morris Library at SIU to try and read up on the man, so I could find out where he was coming from.

I couldn't find out much more about Paul Simon, and that about ended my research. I did consult an ancient Chinese oracle. I spent the rest of the day, then, driving around, trying to find a ride to Springfield. None of my friends were going that way.

ANCIENT CHINESE ORACLE

The leather gaskets on the pump outside the back door were so old that it took seventy five pumps of the metal handle to get five gallons of water. Then the water had to be carried over to the outside bathtub and dumped in. This was repeated until the tub was filled. I took the black macintosh from the closet and spread it out on top of the water so the sun would heat it. On the north side of the tub stands a stump. It is bigger around than you can reach with your arms, and it came from the courthouse lawn in Oxford, Mississippi.

I heard that old Mr. Faulkner used to come into town sometimes and walk around the courthouse talking to retired farmers. I felt sure he must have walked past this particular tree many times. The tree was cut into neat sections nearly three feet high, and it was night in Oxford, so I loaded it up and hauled the huge chunk of wood some seven hundred miles north to my farm.

Back in the house I cleaned and filled the water pipe with fresh water and some of the best Boskydell Boo prunings, which were still young and bright green. I took up some matches and my sly hat. I took up the freshly-filled water pipe and lit it, taking several deep breaths, taking off all my clothes, putting my sly hat on my head, and stepping naked into the sun. I walked over to the Faulkner stump, which now held soap, washcloth, towel, and a cup of iced tea, all within easy reach of the tub. I could see the rust-red roof of the old barn, gray weathered wood, and Fenton's field all deep green with several whiteface cows chewing lespedeza, easy in the shade of a few oaks along the new fence me and Mottsy helped Mr. Fenton build.

Everything seemed in order. I slipped deeper into the water, scooped a hatful over my head, took up the pipe, and only once or twice did I think of what was happening in the capital in the ninety-six degree weather. I felt glad to be exactly where I was at, in the best of all possible worlds. Just then, that is, right there.

The student riots had everyone's mind on what was happening to our country, to our colleges, to our youth. And what to do about them. I was a clean white prune after all that soaking and sun, so I went to seek the advice and opinions of the ancient Chinese Oracle.

I entered the small room with the stained glass window and opened my black leather box with the tarnished brass lock and hinges. The leather was nearly falling apart with age and was soft brown with use. I kept ceremony stuff in it back then. You could say I thought that the ceremony was kind of religious, and it went something like this: First, I sat still and tried as best I could to free my mind of any thought. When a thought came floating by, I didn't try to unthink it, because that would be a thought, too. I sort of let the thoughts go by without paying them too much attention. Like clouds on a distant horizon. A faraway part of the brain. Soon the thoughts came fewer and fewer.

Next, I pumped some well water into a pan put over a wood fire to boil, thinking of the fire as I built it. I went back to the little room and opened the old box, spreading a white brocaded altar cloth with a golden cross on the wooden table, after cleaning up the wood. I took off my shoes and placed the offering in a small silver bowl. I took some ginkgo wood incense, taken from the tea ceremony learned from Alan Watts in California, and put the incense on the burner. I took up the pipe and made an offering in fire, still free from all thought. My head lightened and natural energy flowed through my body and mind.

From a cloth bag I took up three copper coins. A candle gave the only light. I brought in hot water and measured the Japanese green powdered tea into the bowl, whipping it up with a bamboo whisk. After finishing the tea, I prayed for understanding for divine guidance, maybe. I held the copper coins until the cold was gone, thinking about the riots and what could be done to stop them. I threw the coins six times and built a hexagram. I sat as still as I could until my mind was calmer still, then I read the pages indicated by the coins. *The Book of Changes* told me to read all about the well--as if you can go "by the book" in these dangerous times.

The Well

Thus the well is the symbol of that social structure which, evolved by mankind in meeting its most primitive needs, is independent of all political forms. Political structures change, as do nations, but the life of man with its needs remains eternally the same--this cannot be changed. Life is also inexhaustible. it grows neither less nor more, it exists for one and for all. The generations come and go, and all enjoy life in its inexhaustible existence.

However, there are two prerequisites for satisfactory political or social organization of mankind. We must go down to the very foundations of life. For by merely superficial ordering of life that leaves its deepest needs and unsatisfied is as ineffectual as if no attempt at order had ever been made. Carelessness--by which the jug is broken--is also disastrous. *If for instance the military defense of a state is carried to such excess that it provokes wars by which the power of the state is annihilated, this is a breaking of the jug.*
The hexagram also contains a symbolic meaning. Just as water it inexhaustibility as the basic requisite of life, so the 'way of kings'--good government is the indispensable foundation of the life of the state. Place and time may change, but the methods for regulating the collective life of the people remain the same. Evil conditions arise only when the right people are not at hand to execute the plan. This is symbolized by the shattering of the jug before it reached the water.

The Sequence

The setup of a well must necessarily be revolutionized in the course of time. Hence there follows the hexagram of REVOLUTION.

A well must be cleaned out from time to time or it will become clogged with mud. THE WELL, which means a permanent setup, is followed by the hexagram of REVOLUTION, showing the need of changes in long-established institutions, in order to keep them from stagnating. REVOLUTION means removal of that which is antiquated.

The Image

Water over wood, the image of THE WELL. Thus the superior man encourages the people at their work, and exhorts them to help one another.

as revolutions in nature take place according to fixed laws and thus give rise to the cycle of the year, so political revolutions--these can become necessary at times for doing away with a state of decay-- must follow definite laws. First one must be able to await the right moment. Second, one must proceed in the right way, so that one will have the sympathy of the people and so that excesses will be avoided. Third, one must be correct and entirely free of all selfish motives. Fourth, the change must answer a real need. This was the character of the great revolutions of the past by the rulers of Tsang and Wu.

The Lines

Nine at the beginning means wrapped in the hide of a yellow cow.
One should not act thus.

Changes ought to be undertaken only when there is nothing else to be done. Therefore at first the utmost restraint is necessary. One must become firm in one's mind, and the cow is the symbol of docility, and refrain from doing anything for the time being, because any premature offensive will bring evil results.

>Nine in the fifth place means:
>The great man changes like a tiger.
>Even before he questions the oracle.
>He is believed.

A tiger skin, with its highly visible black stripes on a yellow ground, shows its distinct pattern from afar. It is the same path a revolution brought about by a great man; large, clear guiding lines become visible, understandable to everyone... He wins the spontaneous support of the people.

I didn't think that Paul Simon would want to hear much about revolution, and neither did I, for that matter. I finally followed the line of nine at the top and "refrained from doing anything for the time being." Anything except cultivate the garden--vegetables, mint, and herbs.

The candle burned low and I tried to become free from thought again. Lost in ritual, I closed the sacred books, put away the silver bowl, placed the copper coins into their cloth bag, closed the green tea container, cleaned the bamboo whisk and the brown and white bowl, and placed them all carefully in the magic black box.

******

>When your way is *right* before God,
>Everything before you ripen.
>The first seed that could grow
>A faith tree is patience.
>
>Papa John.

WHITE HAIRED WISDOM

Not too long after the riots I won my five dollar bet with that corn picker neighbor of mine, Bob Runion. In Murphysboro, in the Jackson County Courthouse, Judge Rodney Scott legally stopped the proposed rock festival in the township of Makanda. Judge Scott said in part:

1. "That the proposed activity here involved called a Rock Festival, being of recent development and popularity inherently involves an assembly of a large number of people for the purpose of entertainment which assembly engenders crowds within a limited area of space, and which purpose creates emotion, human relations and possible volatile reactions from the close assembly of young people."

2. "That such peculiar nature of this activity raises particular social problems that must be fully explored in advance, fully and carefully provided for..."

3. "That such an activity as a rock festival is a legal activity if properly held under proper conditions to insure the purpose of entertainment as is general accepted under standards of moral conduct by the people of this nation. That from the evidence heard many such activities tend to be improperly held and under such conditions that gathers can only be described as cesspools for the

scum of humanity; that they engender filth, degradation, lawlessness and individuals whose conduct resembles that of the lower animals. Such festivals invite legislation of total abolition as having no socially acceptable purpose."

    First, take some old horseshit. It has to be old, because new shit is too hot and burns the roots. Spread it four inches thick in the bottom of the trench. Then take a hoe and break some of the earth from the pile on one side of the trench back into it, covering the shit. Mix well with the hoe. Then shift more dirt. And mix. If you don't happen to have any horseshit handy, try to find some rotted leaves or mulch from a decayed tree trunk that has crashed in the forest a long time ago, probably having made no sound, since there was no one around to hear it fall.

    What this does is keep the soil loose so that when it rains and the sun shines down, the soil will not bake like a brick around the plants, choking them off. Please keep the soil loose around the base of the plants with a hoe when the are small, especially after a heavy rain.

    The ground has to be broken six to eight inches deep, so don't try to hoe a shallow hole and pop a seed in, because when the plant reaches three feet tall, the main root will be over a foot long. When the root reaches hard-packed soil the plant will stop growing and will become a runt. And who wants to grow runts?

    Since the seeds you have are probably imported, they are used to different sun and soil. The first year your crop might not be taller than your head, but the second generation will be far taller than you can reach, even by jumping, if properly cared for and weather cooperates.

    At the same time the soil is being prepared, soak the seeds in a shallow plate with a couple of layers of wet paper towels. The higher potency the seeds, the better the boo. Boskydell Boo was a mixture of acclimated South American Purple Flowers and Gold from Acapulco.

    After your seeds have soaked for a couple of days, little white clam-neck-like things come creeping out of them, looking for the sun. Plant the seeds in cultivated ground, scratching some loose dirt over them. Water. IN a few days little green matchheads will appear and uncurl into a thin stalk with two green leaves out to the sides. They are smooth. The next pair of leaves are a little jagged along the edges, like they are supposed to be. When three inches high it is necessary to go along and pull up the weaker plants. One year I thought, "Oh, dear, the poor little things! Give them extra water and they will grow strong." They survived, but the truth is that even with extra care a weak plant produces little volume and low quality produce, so *pay attention to the strong* and thin out. I will not say what you can do with the plucked plants.

Just two more important tips. First, pinch the tops of all the plants when the stalk has six pairs of leaves. This will force the plants to send up two main stems instead of one, thereby doubling the yield in one quick pinch. Second, when the plants begin to flower, break over the tops and let them hang, still attached to the plant. This makes the plant realize it is being damaged just at its fullest maturity. This forces the plant to sprout nearly a dozen new tops, which produce the highest potency. Sensimilla, which I called "Super A," was tops. Then the buds and stalk tips were called "A," and then "B" the lower leaves of the female plant, and then "C," the leaves or flowers of the male plant.

Back in '69 no one had even heard of Sensimilla, but I noticed that the plants at the ends of the rows never got pollinated, produced few seeds, and grew fatter and stickier than "A." When shucking off the stalks, my fingers became black with resin and stuck together like they were glued. The Rastafarians had a name for this herb back then. They called it "Lamb's Bread."

Finally, wait, if possible until the first frost or until the Paraquat helicopters are heard in the area, then uproot and hang the plants upside down out of the sun until dry and crisp. There are a few little tricks about pruning, but you can pick them up for yourself. It's a lot of fun, and I'm going out of the business of boo growing for good, so someone has to take over. One tip to the paranoid apprentice grower. A friend once said that if it's going to bother your head a lot worrying about it, it's not worth doing. I guess that might be true about a lot of things.

But listen up. Before you get too deep in the grass, please beware of Beth's letter to Linda found written in round, girlish script on rainbow-colored stationary on the streets of collegetown the winter before the riots. It's really true, so please pay attention. Beth's testimony may convince some readers of the horrors of pot smoking, and the next chapter outlines a deeper dread than Beth could ever imagine.

November 3, 1969

Dear Linda,
    Greetings! Just got your letter today and decided to write back right away since there was so much to tell you about. Wednesday night I went to see Gary Puckett and the Union Gap. They were sooooo great, I really enjoyed them. I wasn't so hip on seeing them because their songs are good (they sing "Woman Woman," "Young Girl," "This Girl is a Woman Now," etc.) But I wasn't crazy about them let me tell you. Gary Pucket has the most fantastic voice)you can't hear it on the records case the band drowns him out). If I were him I would leave the group and sing by myself. Well enough for them, let me tell you about my date. I was fixed up with a 23 year old pharmacy graduate student. His name is Dennis Wong, he is about 5'11 and not bad looking at all. He was really a nice guy--very considerate and all. We had a nice time--talked and listened to records (after the concert), but he will probably never call again. We both thought each other was nice--but that was all, nothing more! Know what I mean? Neither one of us was enchanted with each other. What more can I say about him?

    This weekend was very interesting. I went to Phoenix on Thursday and stayed there until Sunday. Most of the weekend I had a really nice time. We went shopping (I blew another $100!). It was so big and beautiful there I felt as if I were in Chicago (downtown) going shopping with you and Jennifer and Rhonda. I really didn't get very much--a crushed corduroy coat (my spring coats are too light and my winter coat is too heavy! So I got an in-between coat.) a pair of pants, a hand carved coral worry pin (Bought it at my girlfriend's mother's antique shop--it's really beautiful), a work shirt (for grubbing), and a scarf! I really had a lot of fun buying all this junk, (but then I always do!) But my father is going to blow his stack when he sees all my checks! (yuk, yuk!)

I was doing really good on a diet--I had lost 3 pounds since I came here (it's not a lot better than gaining). Well this weekend I ate like food was just invented. Her parents took us to the most exclusive restaurants (really yummy food) and her mother baked tons of stuff for us (all fattening of course!) So I gained six pounds (ugh!) I'm going to have to do something about it cause all my clothes are starting to pull.

We also went to see Arizona State University. It is soo beautiful I can't believe it. We went into the dorms and I was really pisst. Their housing is 1000 times better than ours--it's like living in a hotel, I'm not kidding! But the teachers are supposed to be a lot better here--so I guess I'll continue here--although I might transfer later on (who knows?)

Now that I have told you all the great parts of the weekend--let me fill you in on the less desirable part. Leslie has changed an awful lot since I have last seen her. She has not only changed physically--but she has become very wild. Remember when you told me about Renee trying to pot and how upset you were? Well I couldn't really understand your concern until I found myself confronted with the fact that Leslie smokes pot all the time! I was very upset, but decided it had nothing to do with our friendship and just left it. Well, last saturday night I went to a pot party! In order to get you in the right mood--first let me describe the house it was in. This house was way out in nowhere. It was very old, with squeaky doors, chipped paint, very buggy, poor lighting, no sink in the bathroom, a toilet that didn't flush--a very dilapidated house. It was decorated with posters, paintings, and pictures. All in all, upon first glance I got the feeling as if I were watching a movie. I just could not believe that a place like this really existed. I was actually afraid of this place--I couldn't stand it!

We were the first ones there and since we were only 4 girls I really got scared and thought someone was going to come in and rape us! We were alone for about 15 minutes (it seemed like hours). All of a sudden I see all these tough looking guys drive up on motorcycles and cars. They were so big--I almost pissed in my pants from fear! Well they turned out to be really nice, but nonetheless I kept my distance! We listened to music awhile and then they decided to smoke Keefe (they didn't have pot--but Keefe is practically the same thing only a drop weaker.) Just like in the movies, they made a circle around the table and passed it around from one person to the next--each inhaling some as they went along. They asked me to join but I declined--Thank god they didn't push the issue--I was petrified (I kept thinking we were going to be raped). I always wanted to go to a pot party--just to see if I would stick to my beliefs and not indulge. Well, I found out a lot about myself. I was so repulsed by the whole thing--I got to a point where I could no longer sit there watching them-- so I ran into the bathroom (if you can call this one a bathroom!) and started crying hysterically. (Now you know that I hardly ever--if ever--cry, so you can imagine how upset I was!) About five minutes later Leslie came in to see what was the matter with me. I told her that I did not hate her friends, but I did not agree with their view. I said I was very upset and just wanted to get out of that house. We went out for a ride for awhile and then she told me we had to go back because her boyfriend was coming soon. Since I was beginning to feel better I agreed. It wasn't so bad at the house then, I sat by myself in a corner, and listened to records. Her boyfriend came so I barely saw her and everyone went their own way and ignored me-- which was more than fine with me. I sat there, freezing cold, all by myself, watching others partially stoned and partially drunk.

 All of a sudden, one of the boys decided it would be fun to have a Wesson Oil party. They talked about it before but it was just talk and I didn't think they were really going to do it. Some kids went to buy Wesson Oil and when they came back I realized they weren't joking. By the way--if you don't know what a Wesson Oil party is, let me explain. First everyone takes off all their clothes, then you pour Wesson oil all over the floor and start rolling in it! You feel each other by putting Wesson OIl all over each other's body with your hands (it's supposed to be very sensuous). Afterwards, everyone takes a shower together and they all have an orgy. Being the prude that i am--I thought it was the most perverted and gross thing I had ever heard of. When everyone started taking off their clothes I got really upset and ran out of the house, into one of the cars and sat there crying. Leslie and her boyfriend did not like the idea of it either, so besides me they were the only ones not to participate--but nonetheless they sat there and watched!! They came out to get me several times but I refused to move and so I spent 3 hours in the car! Great Saturday night huh? I thought we would never leave but we finally did. I was very, very upset and just wanted to forget all the vivid scenes in my head but the next day, (after once again gaining my composure) I realized that even though it was a very disturbing experience, I found out an awful lot about myself. I would never want to go through it again, but I am sort of glad that I experienced it because I feel more secure in my convictions about *never* smoking pot!

Leslie and I had a long talk. She apologized and said that we were still friends and when we were together she would refrain herself from this group of kids. I was glad about this as I really think she is a nice kid. If her parents knew they would absolutely die. So would mine as a matter of fact!!!

When I read that you were taking Jennifer to see Simon and Garfunkel I was soooo jealous. I wish *we all* could get together and do *anything!*

Well, gotta go now. Have fun at the concert. How was homecoming? What did you wear there? Anything new?

Bye for now

Love, Beth

PS Write, Write, Write

Within Herbs its personal self
there is a Divine Authority
that gathered itself
within the cranium of man
that show them inspiration
of those God-like qualities
that germinate Divine Consciousness.
The government know on a whole
that herb is not bad.
But if the people of this country
should go and smoke herbs,
the government know that
there won't be no workers
for his country

                              Bongo U

July 2, 1970
POLICE CONFISCATE MARIJUANA CROP
Farm near Carbondale

By Zelah Scalf
Of The Southern Illinoisan

Marijuana, which police said would have been worth more than $30,000 within a few months, was confiscated in a pre-dawn raid on an Indian Creek farm near Carbondale today.

Alex E. Paull Jr., about 28, former operator of the Hippodrome skating rink and dance hall in Murphysboro, was arrested on the premises. Police said Paull claimed ownership of the property.

Paull was charged with possession of marijuana, a felony, and possession of dangerous drugs. He was still in jail in Carbondale pending further interrogation late this morning.

A warrant is to be issued similarly charging a Chicago woman identified as Paull's common-law wife.

Seven Carbondale policemen and Jackson County Deputy Sheriff Leroy Dietz raided the Indian Creek farm about seven miles southeast of Carbondale at 5 a.m. today. the Carbondale policemen were working as county deputy sheriffs under Jackson County Sheriff Ray Dilliner.

Patrolman Charles Malone, first officer to enter the farmhouse, said Paull was alone in the house. The woman is believed to be in Chicago, Maloney said.

A few fully grown marijuana plants surrounded a broken down barn or storage building near the house. Behind the four-room farmhouse, hidden by trees was a patch of marijuana, about 20 by 40 feet.

The police officers were to finish picking the marijuana this morning.

Sgt. Terry Murphy, Carbondale policeman in charge of the raid, estimated the value of the marijuana, had it been allowed to reach full growth, "in excess of $30,000."

At 11 a.m today Sgt. Murphy said police found 30 pounds and two ounces of marijuana, including stalks, seeds and leaves. He listed the value "in excess of $4,000" if the marijuana were processed and sold on the street today.

Carbondale Patrolman Bill Rypkema said the police also found some pills believed to be amphetamines and barbiturates and two containers of white powder, probably opium which is used to process marijuana.

A single firearm was found, a rusted, inoperable shotgun.

Part of the marijuana crop would have been ready for harvest within a month and the remainder would have been grown by the first frost, according to Carbondale patrolman Larry Hill.

Two large stalks of marijuana had been picked and were drying in the yard beside the farmhouse.

Glen Smith, Murphysboro, supervisor of game wardens in district 10, confiscated two red fox skins. Smiths said the absence of an operable gun in the house could mean the animals had been trapped illegally. Smith was to check Paull for a hunting licence.

CHICKENSHIT BOO

One night at the farm my Jamaican baker friend Percy was sitting at the table across from me, shucking seeds from off the stems. "God proved this little comfort," he said, blending the herb with a little tobacco to make it draw better. Percy filled his pipe and I read him a chapter of Boskydell Blue. It goes like this:

I probably wouldn't have met Charlie at all if he hadn't come busting into my bedroom that morning about an hour before sunrise. It's kind of hard to get to know a fellow when you're sleeping in bed all naked and the dog starts barking, and you kind of open your eyes but don't quite get sitting up, and the bedroom door opens so you can see a black leather vest and two black gloves and a thirty-eight police special is aimed right at your face, the barrel hole big as a cannon, and his first words to you are, "DON'T MAKE ANY FAST MOVES AND EVERYTHING WILL BE ALL RIGHT!"

I swung my bare feet to the floor. I could see one man in a uniform with a badge showing. Then there was a submachine gun and other assorted heat coming in all the doors. Walking-around flashlights snapped across the room, talking about looking for roaches. I put on my new red sly hat and asked Charlie if I could go into the other room to find some underwear. He had me firmly by the arm and I saw another man-big gun. They walked me bare-assed through the arcing flashlights. The other six guys were looking in the ashtrays. I was looking through my clean-clothes basket. Charlie kept on saying, "Hurry up! Get some pants on!"

"I'm hurrying as fast as I can." Before you know it I was dressed and outside the door. In the pre-dawn darkness there was a blue pickup barely visible over by the barn-- just exactly where the boo grew tallest last year, because of all the horseshit Old Man Rushing's father Isaac must have shoveled out the west end a long time ago. I could see a crew cut cop about to climb into the barn loft, looking for dope or for naked hippie girls on bare mattresses maybe, and I hollered out across the lawn "Careful, don't wake up no chickens!"

"Fuck the chickens," was the reply.

"If you can handle it!" I shouted back.

Charlie Maloney, the cop who had me, now sat across from me in the bed of a red pickup. Charlie laughed. His buddy drove us both out to the gravel road. Although my hands were held tightly behind my back by a nylon band, I thought of going over the wooden bridge like that one-eyed mail horse did fifty years ago, and making a run for it in the woods, like in the movies. When I saw the way Charlie was looking at me and noticed that the little safety strap over the handle of his gun was left unstrapped, I decided not to give him a chance to shoot me in the back. I rode all the way out to the gravel road with Charlie and was transferred into a waiting car with the sheriff's deputy. Charlie really didn't have much jurisdiction in Boskydell, seeing that he was a Carbondale cop.

When I was on my way to jail, Charlie went back to the farm and pulled up fine Boskydell Boo for the rest of the morning. He thought he was leaving me absolutely booless through the long, hot summer, colorful fall and winter too, but Charlie didn't know everything, you know. I had some "super A" primo buds left in the barn that had gotten the top layer chickenshit-on last fall. The chickens had decided to roost right over the basket of freshly picked flowers. The mess looked like nothing anybody would want to stick their hands into, especially if he had just found twelve pounds, fifteen ounces of boo stalks, some a good yard higher than his head, just like it says in the official search warrant inventory, documented for you so you won't think I'm making all this up. Not only that, but I think they woke the chickens up too, that morning.

When Percy heard my story he began to laugh softly to himself. "Mr. Alec, they've got to charge God about it, because God never wrong putting anything on this earth. Nature never doing anything wrong."

SEARCH WARRANT INVENTORY

I <u>Charles Maloney</u> do hereby state that the following instruments, articles or things were seized from

<u>the farm house and out buildings located 17 of a mile west of the Giant City School on the Boskydell Road, thence 16 of a mile due south on a gravel road south of a bridge across Indian Creek, being the only buildings south of said bridge, in section 11, township 10 South, range 1 West, Makanda Township, Jackson County Ill</u>

in accordance with the command of a certain search warrant issued by the court on the <u>2nd</u> day of <u>July</u> 1970 at <u>5:00 AM</u>.

<u>30 lbs. and 2 oz. of marijuana plants, stalks and seeds divided as follows: 5 lbs. 14 ozs. of tall growing plants of marihuana; 12 lbs. 15 ozs. of dry marihuana stalks; 1 lb of marihuana seeds. Also numerous "roaches" containing marihuana, and a green powdered substance in an oriental can.</u>

Subscribed and sworn to before me this <u>2nd</u> day of <u>July,</u> 1970.

"If they want to do something about that they can go and see Mr. Nature and charge him about that."
"Yeah, but it cost me all that trouble and three thousand dollars!" I said.
"Well, that's justice!" Percy said.
"Justice! Why I wasn't doing anything to bother nobody!"

"Yes, justice," Percy repeated. "Give to Caesar what is Caesar's and that which is God's to God."

GRAND INQUISITION
(play within a play)
The scene is the men's room in the back of the police department in Carbondale, Illinois.
July 2, 1970.

<u>The actors:</u>
Soft patrolman Bill Rypkema
Hard patrolman Charlie Maloney
Sly old fox Terry Murphy, head of narcotics
Fat Smitty, the game warden
Me, and just briefly, Mottsy

<u>Bill</u>: Where did you get all those seeds from?
<u>Me</u>: I brought them with me from California.
<u>Bill</u>: How would you compare your grass with imported?
<u>Me</u>: (proudly) The female tops get you just as high as any grass I ever smoked.
<u>Bill</u>: How can you tell the males from the females?
<u>Me</u>: I told you, the females get higher.
<u>Bill</u>: I mean, how can you tell by looking at them?
<u>Me</u>: The females are more bushy-looking.
<u>Bill</u>: What did you treat it with before you sold it?
<u>Me</u>: I didn't sell any. I just smoked it a lot.
<u>Charlie</u>: (harshly): What did you treat it with?
<u>Me</u>: You don't need to treat it with nothing. All you do is pull it up from the ground and hang it upside down out of the sun like tobacco. When it dries out in a couple of weeks, you smoke it.
<u>Bill</u>: What about that white powder?
<u>Me</u>: If it was in all that painting stuff it's probably bicarbonate my grandfather used to use in New Jersey. I brought a lot of his things out here.
<u>Charlie</u>: You're lying. We'll find out what it is. It's over at the lab right now.

Me: Then let the lab tell you it's bicarbonate.
Bill: Who'd you sell it to?
Me: I didn't sell any. I just like to smoke a lot.
Charlie: Come off it! You had over five pounds growing up there on the hill. You couldn't possibly smoke it all.
Me: Oh yeah? You know what a five gallon paint can is? (Holding my hands two and a half feet from the floor) I had two buckets like that stuffed full of boo last year, and that only lasted me 'til February. I told you before, I really like to smoke a lot.
Charlie: I've never heard of anyone smoking as much as you. We found more roaches at your place than we usually find grass.
Me: That's because I don't like smoking roaches. Some people say they get you higher, but I don't like the way they taste. Bitterish.
Bill: What did you do with them, give them away?
Me: I just threw them in that box you found until somebody came along who was hard up for grass.
Bill: Did you sell them to him?
Me: Nah, I gave them away.
(Sly old fox Murphy writes something down on a pad.)
Bill: Now, when we pulled up the plants, we found these little red pills around the roots. What are they?
Me: Magic.
Bill: No, really, what's in them?
Me: Magic. I told you. I can't tell you exactly, because I don't know, but I was convinced of their magic when they performed the way they were advertised. There was only one picture on the flyer-- a photo of a housewife in England holding a cabbage as big as a bushel basket. The cabbage weighed sixteen pounds. "SHE CAN HARDLY LIFT IT," the flyer said, "BUT THIS IS THE PROUDEST DAY OF HER LIFE."
Bill: All right. Now, what was that green powdered substance in an oriental can?
Me: That ain't dope. It's powdered green tea for the Japanese Tea Ceremony.
Bill: You mean TEA tea?
Me: Yeah, like Lipton's. Only powdered and green and imported. I'm a fancy tea connoisseur.
Bill (confidentially): No, really, what's in the can?

(The door opens. It is Mottsy, smiling. I smile back.)
Mottsy: Excuse me. Ain't this the men's room?
Charlie (shouting): Didn't you see that sign on the door? "Interrogation In Progress?"
Mottsy (handing Charlie the sign): Oh, you mean this?
(Mottsy leaves.)
Fat Smitty: Now, what about those fox hides?
Me: Bought them off a college kid.
Charlie: You're lying! I know when you're lying!
Me (lying): I don't know his name.
Bill: Now, what were you doing with that riot baton in your house?
Me: You mean that sledgehammer handle? You want to know what I was doing with it? A couple of weeks ago I was in Dillinger's feed store to buy some food for my dogs. In walks a Carbondale cop who buys a dozen hickory handles to beat on young heads. I feel kind of sick inside. Something is really wrong with a country when you got to beat people to get them to do what you want. There were only two sticks left, so I bought one of them so I can remember what's going on around here. As much as I love my farm, I still might not want to stay around here if large numbers of people start beating each other up.
Bill: What about the notch on it?
Me: There wasn't no notch on it that I know of. It says "eagle" on the stick and there is a picture of a blue eagle printed on the hickory wood. Jackson County was supposed to be named after Old Hickory, Andrew Jackson. Who did a little massacring of Indians himself. And it all kind of fits in. Too-harsh police create revolutionary consciousness.
Bill: By the way, what side are you on in all of this?
Me: I'm not on any side, and to tell you the truth, I don't even like to live in a place where people are taking sides. That's why I go to Jamaica a lot. I have friends on both sides-- some of my friends are union men and some have long hair. I don't even like to hear about people arming up against each other. What the hell's that going to prove?
Charlie: Now, what about that girl living with you?

Me: There isn't nobody living with me. She's living in Chicago and I'm keeping some of her things for her until she comes back down to go to school.
Charlie: You're lying, fella, and I already told you I don't like it when somebody lies to me! So I will ask you again. What about the girl living with you?
Me: I've already told you. I'm just keeping her things for her.
Charlie: Then what about all that women's underwear folded neatly in those dresser drawers? I'm sure you don't wear them.
Me: Don't be so sure. We all have our secret vices and fetishes when nobody is looking. Even you guys!
Charlie: Not--
Me (interrupting): Sure. Some people like to drink a lot and others like pornography and dirty books. And some people like to beat on others and some roll on the floor for Jesus. But everybody's got something in the closet they don't want nobody to know about. Even you!
(Charlie remains silent. I am put back in jail.)

"But," I said to Percy, "God was good to me after all." That same afternoon when I got free, Mottsy was waiting with a couple of spliffs for the ride back to the farm. We picked up some ribs and we had a symbolic pig roast up on the hill beneath the maple trees flecked white by the twilight sky red with color. We had yellow sweet corn, fresh-picked, steamed in butter, wrapped in foil above the glowing coals. After Mott left I slept outside beneath the night sky. My home felt raped. I heard whippoorwills and frogs by the pond.

Then Charlie Maloney came out to see me again. I wasn't home, but he left a note for me that said "Alex--sorry I didn't find you home. See you some other time. Charles."

I saw Charlie in town the next day. I asked him if he left his dark glasses at the farm. He said yes, and said he might drop by the farm later that night. I wondered why. I went home, and when it was about sunset and Charlie still didn't show, I smoked some cleaned-off chickenshit boo and saddled up Babe. We rode off toward the south.

Babe and Me

When we got to Fenton's field, Babe broke into a full gallop and, as usual, I could not hold her back. The golden grass of summer moved underneath the black horse with the white dog running beside. A lit roach burned through the colors of the setting sun and the clouds turning red, violet, and orange. I heard a motorcycle coming up the dirt road.

With considerable effort I turned the horse into a wide circle and headed back toward the farm. When I came into the yard, Babe started crowhopping and lunging. I was, as usual, in about forty percent control. Across the lawn, under the maple trees on a red motorcycle, was Charlie.

The roach between my lips had gone out, so I slipped it into my mouth with my tongue. When the acrid taste went away I moved it up beside my gum like a pinch of snuff. Herb made Charlie crazy, I told myself, and I didn't want to take any chances.

Charlie sat on his bike with one leg crossed over the metal gas tank. He wore a khaki shirt open in front, showing his badly-scarred belly. A bulged showed out at the hip because Charlie's always got his heat with him. His motorcycle looked like a tin kid's toy from atop the black walker. Babe was all sweating and dying to run out like all hell, all excited and farting, neck held in a tight arc like in the picture.

"Hi, Alex."

"Hi, Charlie." I crossed my leg over the McClellon saddle and looked down at him. Now, I know that everyone from my lawyer, Jimmie Lawder, to people who think Charlie ain't nothing but a pig, tell me I shouldn't have talked to him, but you can't always go by what your friends think. I slid off the saddle and said, "Let me tie her and I'll be right with you."

I tried to tie the black horse to a tree in the yard but she started pulling back hard. I had to run behind her, chucking softly with my mouth, to make her ease up on the halter before she snapped the reins. She had gotten tangled up in a fence once, and I had tried to cut the reins to free her, so one rein was cut almost through in one place. Any hard jerk would part the leather. When I rode Babe I used to choke up on the reins anyway, giving me more power over her and bypassing the weak place.

Since Charlie had come into my life in the middle of the night with a black leather vest, big gun, and gloves, I figured he may be some kind of evil. It was possible I could get him riding over Fenton's field until the rein broke, the Tennessee Walker carrying him all wild and galloping until she came to a ravine or a washout, jumping, leaving Charlie in the air and helpless, crashing to the ground. But first I wanted to be sure Charlie deserved this natural revenge. I said a quiet prayer that I could learn more about him and do the right thing.

Charlie got off his bike and shook my hand like an old friend. "I see you made it up here," I said to him.

"That dirt road of yours is pretty rough after that rain yesterday."

"If I can make it up in that old truck, you shouldn't have any trouble on a dirt bike."

"No trouble," Charlie said. He looked over to the barn where Babe was beginning to wander off. "You just leave her to walk around like that?"

"Sure, she can't go nowhere. Neighbor's fence to the south and west, and rock bluff on the east." I pointed. "Besides, who do you think keeps the grass mowed around here? But I'm going to have to get behind the mower to level off them weeds, because she don't eat no weeds." We grinned. "Do you like to ride horses?"

"I've done it some," Charlie said.

I remembered that I had some coffee hot on the stove for when I got back from riding. "Do you want some coffee? I've got some hot?"

"Sure, I'll take a cup."

We walked past the handpump where the tallest plant had grown tall and full as a Christmas tree until yesterday. I was inside the backdoor with Charlie about to come in when I remembered that handful of chickenshit boo on the kitchen table. In plain sight. I turned back toward Charlie, who was right behind me. "Let's have coffee out on the lawn," I said. "The house is kind of a mess and I'm a little embarrassed over it."

"There's no need to be embarrassed," he said kindly. He turned to go and sit on the grass. I hoped he liked his coffee black because I was out of milk and some of Charlie's friends had dumped all my flour, sugar, and powdered cleanser all together in a pile on the floor. Looking for needles, I guess. We both drank the coffee black, Charlie and me sitting on the lawn with the dark coming on.

"You really got a nice place here. I'd sure like to have a place like this to come home to, after working in town all day."

"Yep," I said, puckering my lip around a little so the roach wouldn't fall out of my mouth. "This place takes all my troubles away when I'm here."

"Everybody needs a place to get away to. That's why I do so much hunting and trapping when the season is in."

"What do you trap?"

"Beavers."

"I didn't know there were any beavers around here," I said.

"There's a lot of them around here. They just don't like to be close to civilization, so you have to walk a few miles through the woods to get to them."

"You mean right here in Jackson County?"

"Sure. You know where the train tracks run through Boskydell?" Charlie asked.

"Yes."

"All you got to do is walk up the tracks toward town and there is a big hutch off in a slough to the east side."

"What kind of fur do they have?"

"Kind of a deep chocolate brown. Sometimes tinged with red."

"Sounds pretty as hell," I said.

"They sure have fine pelts," he agreed.

"I'll have to go and take a look at them, first chance I get. Thanks for telling me about them."

"Don't mention it. Say, listen, Alex," Charlie said, his voice becoming a little confidential. "Say, if I knew a couple of days ago what I know now, I probably wouldn't have busted you. I smoke a joint now and then myself. But I never met anyone who smoked as much as you."

"I do enjoy it," I said, surprised at his candor. "You know those stalks you found out by the barn? They were all from last year," I said.

"Those high plants, like the one by the well?" he said. "If the were wholesaled on the street today, do you know what they would bring?"

"No," I said. "I don't go near the street with any."

"About three hundred bucks each. And how many plants do you think we pulled up?"

"I don't know. I never bother to count them."

"Well, fifteen hundred times three hundred is forty-five thousand dollars!"

"Shucks. I never know it would be worth that much."

"If the all got as big as that one plant, it would."

"Well, money isn't everything," I said. I was still surprised that Charlie had admitted smoking boo sometimes, and I was also careful for any lie or deceit. Many of my friends think you can never trust a pig. I'm just not so sure that Charlie's a pig, that's all.

"If I were you Alex, I'd get Dick White for my attorney. He's the best around."

"I know he is, Charlie, but he wants fifteen hundred dollars up front. I don't mind working to pay for my mistake, but I don't want to have my mother put up her house for mortgage or to bother all my friends. Everybody needs money these days."

"But you might have to do some time."

"Not me, You can tell by the way I live up here." I waved my arm around, indicating the farm. "I couldn't last six months in a jail, not to think about a year. I'd leave my horse, my farm, and everything I loved to find a place where I wouldn't have to live in a cage."

"Then I wouldn't take any chances," Charlie said. "If you have to borrow the money from your mother, at least you will have the best lawyer. And take it from me, Dick White is the best."

"Shit. You know what bothers me, Charlie? I'm making over a hundred and fifty clear a week and I have people who could lend money to me. So I get the dough and hire the best. And maybe somebody from the north side of town ain't got no money. I shouldn't get a better chance at justice than anybody else, just because I can come up with the money."

"Yeah, that bothers me too sometimes. But you got to protect yourself as best you can."

"Tell me something, Charlie. Most everyone said that part of the money goes into other people's pockets, so they will go easy on me. But I think that sooner or later somebody would get caught at it."

"No, that's not it. You see, the judicial system ought to be separated from political offices. If we were really concerned with justice. The state's attorney is thinking about his record. He wants that judge's seat real bad, and doesn't want to lose any cases right now. And Dick White doesn't lose. The state's attorney will want to make a deal out of court. Just wait and see."

"I never thought about it that way. Thanks for the tip," I said.

"Don't mention it. If you don't mind, I might stop by and see you again sometime."

"Feel free, Charlie. I like company. Enjoyed talking with you. No need to rush off."

"It's dark and I've got to go. I barely made it up your road in good light." Charlie stomped his motorcycle to life and eased his way down the rutted dirt road, trying to wave back at me at the same time. I could hear the boards rattling in the bottom when he cleared the old wooden bridge. I told myself I had to find a way to get the best this system had to offer. Rather than the worst.

HERE COMES THE JUDGE

"Your name is Alex Paull?"

" Yes, your honor."

"And you are now appearing before this court on your own motion this morning in the company of the state's attorney. And for what purpose do you now appear?"

"Your honor," the state's attorney, Richard Richman, said. "Prior to coming to court this morning, and on earlier occasions this week, Mr. Paull has been in touch with me, and I have advised him that I could not discuss his case with him until he obtained counsel. He has advised me that he desires to waive an attorney and desires to waive indictment and to be arraigned following that. I am at a loss, quite frankly, to tell him anything, and it would be up to the court to decide whether he should be permitted to do this. He is of above-average intelligence and he is a college graduate. I believe he could knowingly and understandingly waive his right to counsel, and could waive indictment."

"Is there anything that the state's Attorney has said that you are in disagreement with, Mr. Paull?"

"No, sir."

"And you are not now nor have you ever been under any care for psychiatric disorders or mental disorders?"

"No, sir," I said, "I am in full control of my faculties." I was proud of this.

"And you understand that these charges against you are felony charges? The difference between a felony and a misdemeanor is that in a felony charge, upon conviction, it is possible to have imposition of sentence to servitude in a penitentiary. Do you understand that?"

Jail! "Yes, I understand that."

"Before any further proceedings," the state's attorney said, "I feel he should be further advised of his right to counsel."

"I have discussed my case with counsel," I said.

"You have discussed your case with the counsel of your own choice?" asked the judge.

"I have, your honor."

"And this is a private attorney?"

"Yes, sir."

"And you were required to pay for those services of that attorney and were willing and able to pay for them?"

"Yes," I said.

"Then I will accept your waiver of attorney and your written waiver of indictment. You may read these and if you desire, you may sign them and tender them to the court."

I signed and tendered the instruments.

"How do you plead to the charge that on July 2. 1970, in Jackson County, Illinois, you did commit the offense of illegal possession of narcotic drugs, in that you knowingly possessed and had under your control otherwise than authorized in the Uniform Narcotic Act of the State of Illinois then in force and effect, more than 2.5 grams of a certain narcotic drug, to wit; Cannabis Sativa L. (Commonly known as marijuana) in violation of Section 22-40, Chapter 38 of Illinois Revised Statutes, 1969. How do you plead to the charge, either guilty or not guilty?"

" I want to plead guilty with an explanation."

"I am going to give you an opportunity to be heard on this particular thing, to state anything you want, but I will not now or ever accept any conditional pleas. You either plead guilty or you plead not guilty. Whichever plea you wish to tender to this court, I am now ready to hear."

"I wish to plead guilty, your honor."

And then I read this statement:

"Now, a lot of my friends tell me I was a fool for not fighting them, and that I should never have copped out and pleaded guilty. What you need to know is that when Charlie woke me and the chickens up that morning, every shell that served as an ashtray in my house had more than several roaches in them, as did the coal bucket. On a chair next to me in the bedroom was a large colander filled with freshly thinned out little herb plants drying, and on a window ledge in the front room was a small wooden box that held hundreds of roaches that I saved up to give to some needy head. In my study above the fuse box was a few sweet female tops of the best of Boskydell Boo '69 that I had lost, and that Charlie's friends found for me. On a washstand near the mirror was a one pound coffee can nearly full of seeds I had yet to plant. Just outside the back door, right next to the white pump, grew a five foot high herb tree, just as full and green as a Christmas tree, due to the proper pruning of female tops. The proud plant had volunteered itself in that exact spot early in the spring, and who was I to go against nature? Did I have "prehemiency" over nature?

In a field just north of the house, a covey of policemen and the fat lady reporter with sunglasses, named Zela, found and picked fifteen long rows of herbs that were all carefully cultivated, thinned, and fertilized. It was a regular tea party. Later that same afternoon, all of the crop was on the first floor beneath the jailhouse in Murphysboro, the county seat.

I was there in the jailhouse, too, while the sheriff, Raymond Dillinger, processed me. I walked over to the two pillowcases taken from my bed that morning were now brimming full and packed fat with bright green boo. I sniffed them loudly.

'Sure smells fine, Raymond,' I said to the sheriff. 'You can't say I ain't a good farmer. Why, you can't even reach the tops of them.' I jumped up a little, but could not reach the tops of last year's boostalks, all bundled and stacked in a corner of the county safe like so much sugar cane at the Montego Bay market.

I had on my sly hat, and Raymond and all those official folks laughed. I laughed too. The deputy didn't have a hold of my arm by then. He must have known I was too smart to run, and that I wouldn't want to make anyone look bad by getting away.

So, after all this, I couldn't find it in my heart to plead not guilty. Later on I checked to see that they had the proper legal papers to come up and harvest my crop for me, so what more could I do?"

"How do you plead?" asked the judge, interrupting my reverie.

"Guilty, your honor."

"Now, Mr. Paull. You have offered to me, after a full and complete and extensive colloquy of your respective rights, a pleas of guilty to the criminal felony charge before this court. I now advise you that you may withdraw your plea of guilty and have that question of guilt or innocence tried before this court and a jury. In addition to the right of counsel and the right of presentation to the grand jury, and the right to withdraw your plea, I advise you that you have a right to require the presence of all the witnesses on behalf of the State, and for them to testify under oath, and subjecting themselves to your examination, or your attorney's, if you desire. Do you understand?"

"Yes sir. I do understand."

"You have advised the court that you have no limitations as to your capacity to understand the charges, no limitations to your capacity to assist counsel if a trial is held, and we have discussed every one of your rights. Now, in addition to everything else, I am going to now require that the state's attorney's office on the record give you the full benefit provisions of a conviction."

"Your honor," the state's attorney said, "Before I do that I would like to make a short statement. I would like for the record to show very clearly that I have very carefully avoided any negotiations with this defendant, with regard to a possible sentence. The defendant has expressed some interest in what I might recommend, and I have told him on several occasions, and I am sure he will verify it, that I have refused in any way to negotiate."

"The court accepts your statement. And we now ask that you, in detail, read from the statute."

"Your honor, the statute provides for this particular offense that the penalty shall be a fine of not more than five thousand dollars and imprisonment in the penitentiary for a period not less than two years nor more than ten years. This is a probational offense."

The judge said, "And you said a fine of not more than five thousand dollars and imprisonment? Is this a mandatory imprisonment?"

"No, I would assume that it should read 'either/or,' in this particular case."

"You are advising the defendant that the maximum fine would be five thousand dollars and that the minimum term if a penitentiary sentence is imposed is two years and the maximum sentence is ten years. Now, is there any question about what the statute says, in your mind, Mr. Paull?"

AND BE IT FURTHER REMEMBERED THAT THE ABOVE NAMED DEFENDANT, ALEX PAULL, AGAIN APPEARED IN OPEN COURT BEFORE THE HONORABLE JUDGE EVERETT PROSSER, ONE OF THE ASSOCIATE JUDGES OF THE FIRST JUDICIAL CIRCUIT OF THE STATE OF ILLINOIS, JUDGE PRESIDING, ON THE LAST DAY OF JULY, A.D. 1970, FOR THE PURPOSE OF HEARING IN AGGRAVATION AND MITIGATION.

On that day, the judge leaned forward on the bench and said to me, "Mr. Paull, on the 9th day of July, 1970, you appeared before this court, and after an intensive colloquy between you and the court, the court received your plea of guilty, charging you with illegal possession of a narcotic drug in excess of 2.5 grams, a felony. We have advised you of all your constitutional rights, is that true, Mr. Paull?"

"Yes, that's right."

"Now, are you prepared this morning to offer any evidence that you desire, to this court, in mitigation of these charges? I am in accordance with your request made, accepting your application for a hearing on petition for probation. You have orally made such a petition, and you made it in the absence of counsel, and we are going to consider that. Are you ready with your evidence?"

"Yes, sir," I said, taking a deep breath.

WHEREUPON ALEX PAULL, THE DEFENDANT, PROCEEDED AS FOLLOWS:

"Your honor, I have made it my habit to look as closely as I can at whatever situation I find myself in. I believe, your honor, that you and I care concerned with the same basic thing, and that is our concern for the truth. I am a writer, and I try to make my words fit the truth. I think it is one of the responsibilities of the court to see that the words spoken fit the truth as closely as possible. Understanding that meaning is often obscured by words but understood and comprehended in context.

"When I was called upon to address the court as 'your honor,' I was concerned about what honor means. If the court would allow, I would like to quote what one man has to say about honor. 'It is that knowledge and wisdom, far from being one, have oftentimes no connection, but knowledge dwells in heads replete with thoughts of other men, and wisdom in minds attentive to their own.' James Fenimore Cooper.

"In other words, your honor, what this man, this attorney, James Fenimore Cooper is saying, is that you, as a justice, are called upon to make decisions daily about the future of individual persons brought before you. And this depends on your own individual interpretation of the law and the circumstances of each individual case."

"As far as I understand," the judge said kindly, "That is the responsibility of the presiding judge. You may proceed."

"Thank you, your honor. In my search for ways of looking at what is occurring in the courtroom today, I believe I came to a better understanding of how the judicial process works. The system of laws enacted by our legislature is for the protection of individual citizens, and when a case comes before the court, the court is in some measure obliged to decide upon the law, in order to decide upon the case."

"I think that is the procedure," said the judge.

"Thank you, your honor. Uniting the trial of the law with the trial of the individual, the legislature is thereby protected from what we call personal interest. I believe the principle upon which my penalty rests is whether my behavior has caused harm to myself or to the society which you are sworn to protect. I have reason to believe that certain inferences about marijuana use may not be applicable in my case, but I don't know if the court is willing to accept--"

"We will hear whatever statement you wish to make," said the judge. "I am giving you complete carte blanche to say whatever you desire to say."

"Your honor, as stated in the probation report, I told the officer that I had at time smoked marijuana, and I had continued under the influence of the herb for long periods of time. And it did not interfere with my work, in terms of painting."

"Now, Mr. Paull," said the judge. "You are trying to explain to me that you have used this particular marijuana, but you are not trying to say that you recommend that, are you?"

"No, sir, I am not at all."

"You are explaining your own conduct?"

"Yes, sir, because I think the principle behind the law is that the drug leads the individual to certain moral irresponsibility, and leads to certain kinds of anti-or a-social behavior."

"But not necessarily so, as regards to your own case?"

"In my particular case, that is correct. The herb seems to slow down the time process, that is what my--"

"That is the way it affects you?" The judge shooed a fly from his face.

"Yes sir. That is the way it affects me. I am also working on a novel which I feel is of literary competence, and which is not distorted by my use of marijuna."

"You have asked that I consider your application for probation as part of the penalty for conviction, which is based upon your own plea of guilty?"

"Yes."

"And you have admitted to the court by your own statement that you have been a habitual user of this narcotic drug. You have advised the court that, in your opinion, the use of that narcotic drug has not created an antisocial condition. Nor has the use of that drug caused you to inflict injury socially or otherwise upon the society.

"I am not going to quarrel," he went on, "with whatever offer you have made in this regard. But I am particularly interested in your attitude about the fact that this drug has been declared to be an illegal drug by the lawmakers of this state.

"You have entered your plea of guilty to use of this drug. As a matter of fact, I think the charges were that you were growing this drug and that you had a considerable quantity of this drug. From the report that you have made to the probation officer, who is present in court, you said that if your application for probation is accepted, that you will not engage in the growing of this narcotic drug. You will not purchase the narcotic drug. I take it that though you have a quarrel with the adequacy of the judgement of the Illinois legislature that it is a dangerous drug, that you will abide by its decision so long as that law remains on the books of the State of Illinois. Is that true, Mr. Paull?"

"Yes, sir," I said.

"All right, sir. We accept that statement. Now, is there anything you wish to offer?"
WHICH CONCLUDED DEFENDANT'S PRESENTATION OF EVIDENCE IN SUPPORT OF APPLICATION FOR PROBATION. AND WHEREUPON, PRE-SENTENCE INVESTIGATION WHICH WAS ADMITTED IN EVIDENCE AND MADE A PART OF THIS RECORD IS AS FOLLOWS, TO-WIT:

I. <u>OFFENSE</u>
____Illegal Possession of Narcotic Drugs.

II. <u>Defendant's Statement and Attitude</u>

Alex Paull was interviewed by Jackson County Adult Probation Officer. At the time of the interview Alex seemed to be nervous and somewhat excited. He was concerned about whether or not he might be sent to the penitentiary. Alex stated that he had used pot (marijuana) for quite some time and that he had chain smoked it at times. He said that he is unable to see or feel that it has been harmful physically or mentally to him; that while under the influence of marijuana he is capable of performing any precise act that he could otherwise perform without the marijuana drug. He said that he never sold any marijuana nor had he encouraged or enticed anyone to use it or any other type of drug. The reason he grew his own marijuana was that it was too expensive to buy and he didn't like to deal with people who sold drugs. Also that when anyone asked his opinion as to whether or not marijuana was harmful, he always told them he didn't believe it was harmful to you physically but it might be possible that you could develop a mental dependency for the drug and that it could be harmful to you to the extent that it was illegal and you could get into serious trouble by using marijuana. He also stated that he believed that the reason marijuana was illegal was due to the fact that the people who dealt in tobacco and alcohol products had so much lobby power in government that they did not want to see marijuana legalized because it would hurt their business.

He said that if given probation, he would promise that he would never raise or cultivate any more marijuana plants unless it becomes legal to do so. He said that he wanted to continue to live in Southern Illinois on his small farm and to be accepted by the people of the community.

III. Prior Record
    A. Juvenile Delinquencies
        none could be found
    B. Adult Arrest Record
        no convictions
    C. Detainer
        none

IV. Education
    A. Eight (8) Years at George G. White School
    B. Four (4) Years at Pascack Valley High School at Hillsdale, New Jersey
    C. Two (2) Years Jr. College, Diablo Valley Cal.
    D. Two (2) Years at San Francisco State College

V. Home and Neighborhood
    Alex Paull's home is a small farm south of Carbondale located in Makanda Township.

VI. Interests and Activities
    writing and travel

VII. Military History
    none

VIII. Health
    Good. Above average intelligence and mentally stable

IX. Summary

Alex Paull is a white male who has a college education and is working as a housepainter 5 days a week. He has never had any bad trouble with the law until now. Alex seems to think that the marijuana law is wrong, and that the drug should be made legal, but he stated that he would obey the law from now on and refrain from cultivation of cannabis. From all reports, he seems to be a hard working young man.

I think that Alex Paull would do good on probation, and I would recommend probation.

Signed,
Charles Brantley
Adult Probation Officer

An aside: What actually happened was when Mr. Brantley finished asking all his questions, we go to know each other a little, and he leaned forward over his desk and said, confidentially, "Now, Alex, after all the trouble you've seen over marijuana smoking, would you smoke it again?"

I answered him without thinking. "Well, let me put it this way. I'm not going to grow it. And I won't have any of it in or around my house, or on my person. But if I'm at a party or something, and someone passes it my way, I'm surely not going to turn my head away from it."

He seemed relieved. He talked to me like an old friend. "I'm going to recommend probation for you, even though I will have to stand a little static from some of the boys around here. I have a reputation for being a conservative ex-state policeman. But you know what convinced me to recommend probation in your case?"

I was feeling lightheaded with relief. "What?" I asked.

"Your answer to that last question, Alex. You told me repeatedly that you thought marijuana was harmless and that you enjoyed it, and if you would have told me you would not ever smoke pot again, you would be lying. Let me tell you something, Alex-- I don't like people who lie to me. I recommend they go to jail."

In order to get probation recommended, therefore, I had to promise to smoke grass again. I have not broken that promise.

WHEREUPON THE STATE'S ATTORNEY PROCEEDED TO MAKE RECOMMENDATIONS TO THE COURT AS FOLLOWS:

"May it please the court, I have seen the presentense investigation and report prepared by Mr. Brantley, and the recommendations contained therein for probation. I am sure the court is aware, and increasingly aware, as well all are, in the judicial system in Jackson County particularly, of the tremendous drug problem that has existed for some time and which is getting more and more serious. As the court indicated in its colloquy with the defendant, neither the court nor I made the law or suggested the penalties that might be imposed. And whether we like it or not, we can't be concerned with the correctness of that law in our judicial system. It might be that the maximum penalty for the possession of marijuana is out of proportion to the offense."

Another aside: The state's attorney knows very well that smoking the herb is not related to the serious drug problem. He and I talked about it in his office before my premature harvest.

In court, the state's attorney continued. "The court, I think, can't say that either. It may be some time in the future the law will be changed, but it isn't and it has not been changed as yet. I am really at a loss, your honor, to make a recommendation in this case. I don't think that would be fair. I know that the policy of the court in the past and my policy in the past with regard to possession of marijuana. I think in this case we have a larger amount. We also have an older person. Regarding the report, I have talked with Mr. Paull many times in the last few years. I know the gentleman rather well. He is very likable. I don't think sending him to the penitentiary is going to rehabilitate him. I don't think he needs rehabilitation in the usual sense of the word, the usual penal sense. But I think the nature of the offense, this particular offense, calls for more stringent penalties than the court has been imposing or that my office has been recommending in the past. I would recommend, your honor, I throw this out for your consideration, that Mr. Paull be placed on probation for three years, that he be fined three thousand dollars, and that he be sentenced to the county jail for thirty days.

"Now, I think I have admonished you as to all of your rights," the judge said to me. "I have previously accepted your plea of guilty and entered judgement thereon and reserved the issuance of sentence, and I have given you full and adequate time to submit evidence in mitigation of your charges. I have given you and I have given the state's attorney's office opportunity to submit any evidence that they desire. I am in the same condition that the state's attorney finds himself when he tries to make a recommendation to this court.

"The state's attorney says he cannot avoid the fact that his activity is not limited to the confines of The People of the State of Illinois v. Alex Paull, because what we do here may have a direct burden and direct effect upon other cases before this court. I want you to understand that the state's attorney, who represents the prosecuting side of this court, and this court, have the responsibility, after having determined guilt, to fix punishment. We cannot ignore the fact that <u>what the court does here may in some wise influence others who are not present in court today</u>. That being so, I want you to understand that that is part of this sentence.

"Now I am not going to quarrel with you and I'm not going to give you further opportunity to make further statements to me about the reason why or the sufficiency of the judgement of the Illinois legislature in determining what is and what is not a punishable crime. I am going to say to you that that has nothing to do with the judgement of this court. I take the law as it is handed down to me. I do not make a judgement as to whether or not there is medical evidence adequate to sustain the penalties, whether or not there is in fact a failure on behalf of science to have completely exhausted what should be the basis of a narcotic drug test. I take it as I find it in the statute. I have taken your pleas as you have given it to me in court, and I think more than anything else, we want nothing done here to work against the administration of the law. The state's attorney and I are both obligated to stand for the protection of The People of the State of Illinois and of Jackson County.

"And if my treatment of you is at all personal, then I have violated my responsibilities, just as much as Mr. Richman would have violated his responsibilities. With that rather lengthy background, I am going to accept your application for probation. I want you to know that as far as I can remember, and I have been a judge now for some twenty-six years, this is the first time I have, even under the strength of this kind of record, accepted such an application for probation, but I am accepting it. I am going to fix your sentence at your being placed on probation, and I am going to enlarge upon what Mr. Richman previously recommended. I am going to make that term of probation five years. The reason being, Mr. Paull, the length of sentence for this charge is such that I want you to have a responsibility to Mr. Brantley and to his court. I ask your cooperation, just as I have listened patiently to your request, I now want you to be a model citizen for the benefit of others in this community.

"I am advising you that your terms of probation are to include the payment of a fine in the amount of three thousand dollars, and the costs of this proceeding. I am going to advise you that you will comply with every request made by Mr. Brantley's office as regards reporting and any other individual requests that he might make of you. Do you understand all of this?"

"Yes, sir, I do."

"All right, now I am going to further advise you that if at any time during the terms of your probation you are brought before this court or any other court for infringement of the statutes of the federal government or any other local statute, it immediately makes possible to revoke your probation and the imposition of a sentence within the maximum limits of the statute for your plea of guilty to a felony charge. You understand that, Mr. Paull?"

"Yes, sir, I do."

And it was all over. Almost. Except for Sheriff Dillinger still had my black box in his jailhouse safe

SHERIFF DILLINGER HELPS ME TO GET A HEAD

Sheriff Dillinger was not a young man. He was a lean, mild mannered Southern Illinois ex-farmboy. He walked slow. Talked even slower. Sometimes he even said "goldarnit." Sheriff Dillinger is tall, his hair is white, and he knew by first name almost everybody who had lived in the county of Jackson for more than a couple of years. Not counting most of those university folks, of course. Most of the time he wore a western hat on a head of thinning hair.

Raymond Dillinger is just as friendly as a man can be. He knew me by my first name, too, because he'd seen me at all those stop-the-rockfest meetings. Although he may have thought my hair was a little long, he pumped my hand just as hard as anybody's, and gave me the same easy smile, looking for a vote all year around. Even after all my trouble with the law I would have still voted for him, too, if I put any stock in voting. Which I don't. But Sheriff Dillinger still had my black ceremony box locked up in his walk-in safe.

Some weeks after all the trouble had settled, I was still trying to get back my sacred box, and my hoes, too, from out of the jailhouse safe. One fine day I went to into the sheriff's office. He had an ancient white oak desk turned golden with age, a rolltop antique with lots and lots of pigeonholes, which seemed to need organizing. I told Sheriff Dillinger politely that I wanted my black box back, because there wasn't no dope in it and my lawyer, Jimmie Lawder, said I could have it back.

"All right," he said. We walked over to the big safe built into a wall. He opened the heavy black iron door, taller than he and covered with golden scrolls and filigree. We stepped inside. He turned on the light. There in a corner was not only my black box but also the best of Boskydell Boo 1970, all stacked up in the corner, along with the two fat pillowcases taken from my clean clothes basket and still stuffed full of bright green herbs starting to wilt. There was also what looked like a couple of hot tenspeed bikes along one wall, and, in a corner with the soil still on them, were my hoes.

The old sheriff took my black box off the top shelf. He waved an arm at all my herb, twelve pounds of herbstalks bending their heads low at the ceiling of the safe. "I just don't know what I'm gonna do with all this grass," he said. "I guess I better take it out somewhere in the country and burn it. The state's attorney says I can't burn it in the furnace here in the courthouse basement, because all the men up in the jail on the roof!"

We both laughed at that. We both knew that the jail windows look out onto the roof. All the windows were open because it was summertime and the smoke would drift from the chimney and give all those poor guys in the slammer a smile on their faces. What kind of punishment would that be, I ask you?

"Why not just give it back to me, sheriff?" I asked. "I promise I'll take it out in the country and burn it up, all of it, little bit at a time!"

Kind Sheriff Dillinger laughed some more, but he was sorry, he couldn't do that. He leaned over and opened my black box, still smiling. He shuffled around inside the thing with his hands. "Guess I better check this out, anyway," he said.

"Don't worry, Sheriff. There's no dope in there," I said, as he pushed the silver bowl around and took out the container of green tea with oriental writing. I looked into the box too, but my heart started pumping so hard I thought he might hear it, because there was a fat white business-size envelope in the box that I didn't put there. The sheriff asked me about the green tea, and I assured him it was drinking tea. He closed the box, and I said, "Thanks a lot, Sheriff!" as calmly as I could.

I grabbed my hoes in the other hand. He told me to behave myself in a tone of voice I could clearly see that he meant it kindly. As a neighbor or brother would, perhaps. I felt like jumping two steps at at time down the front sandstone steps. Made of sandstone quarried in Boskydell, I bet. When I got to the old truck, I carefully put the black box on the seat beside me and looked around to see if anyone was watching.

When I saw I was alone, I opened the box. Inside the white envelope was what appeared to be some of the finest female boo flowers from 1969, my "Super A" that I had stashed someplace and forgot where. Charlie's men went and found my fine female tops for me. I wanted to be sure, so I pulled out onto a deserted dusty gravel road outside of Murphysboro and I stopped the old truck beneath a huge oak tree. Beneath the spreading green branches overhead, I tore a four by six inch piece from a brown paper sack and rolled me a terrific Jamaican-style spliff, fat as a banana on one end, funneling right on down to a small circle of brown paper on the small end of the cone. I fired away, walking out into green fields of soybeans, careful not to damage a single plant.

The sun was beginning to set the clouds themselves on fire. "Why, thank you, Sheriff!" I said aloud, the spirits of setting sun now as gold and red as my eyes. "With thanks and praises to the Most High," I added. I took in a deep breath of sweet country air, saw the fireflies darting in the shadows of the deeper woods between tree trunks of hickory and white oak, honeysuckle incensing the air, birds diving for night cover among the bushes, and the sun falling slowly over the horizon.

I thought about giving to Caesar what is Caesar's, as Percy suggested. And giving to God what is God's. I still think about that.

'Papa'
John Hall

Photograph by Larry Jasud

MANGO SMILES

Jamaican hillbillies bounced into the Montego Bay market at night in the back of flatbed trucks, twenty-five and thirty at a time. The hillbillies were packed in with their baskets full of mangoes and oranges, stalks of green bananas and plantain, lumpy sacks of yams, delicate bunches of fresh-cut peppermint, and perhaps some wet, or semi-refined sugar in brown and sticky lumps wrapped in shiny green banana leaves.

It's a bleary-eyed six-thirty on a Saturday morning back in the late '60's, before Bob Marley and Michael Manley days, too. I saw no other white person. Pure black. I looked around the market, feeling as obvious and out of place as a marshmallow in a coal bucket. A small man stood near a concrete vegetable stall. He had two large burlap sacks and a woven basket next to him. He wore a peaked baseball cap of wide ribbed red corduroy. A neatly brushed beard scattered with white falls to his chest.

"Now don't try and cheat me, girl," he said. "I might be needing to buy some of your yellow yams today." He looked directly into the big woman's brown eyes when he spoke. His own eyes shone with affection.

"Oh, no, Mr. percy, you know I never ask you too much." She put an extra mango in his basket.

"That's right. Now please let me see your yellow yams. I need about forty pounds of it. how much, please?"

"Seventeen cents per pound." Percy nodded his head. She handed him the scale to hold by a chain. The face of the old brass scale was darkened by time, the handworn edges shone soft gold. One at a time, she put in roots tick as a wrist, twice weighing out twenty pound yellow yam stacks. The shiny brass needle wobbled at twenty three the first time, and then at twenty one, after she exchanged a lighter yam for a larger one.

PERCY

"Lovely yams," Percy said, appreciating the extra pound. The woman looked off into space, her lips moving silently as she figured. When she told him how much, Percy took a blue ball-point pen from his shirt and began to write on the light brown palm of his left hand. "That's right," he said.

He paid her, carefully counting the money twice to make sure. He stooped to help her pile yams into his burlap sack. "Thank you, my dear," he said, smiling all the while. Percy straightened up, holding the neck of his full sack of yams. He looked around and saw me watching him. His wide smile divided his beard from his mustache. He walked up to me, looked straight into my eyes, offered me his brown hand, and said, "Howdeedoo?" I took his hand.

"And how are you enjoying your visit to Jamaica?"

"Very much. You live in a beautiful country. My name is Alex."

"Mine is Percy Thompson."

"You sure got lots of roots," I said, motioning toward the fat sack. "Big family?"

"No, a restaurant. And a bakery, too. In Mount Salem. Have you eaten one of our lovely mangoes as yet? They are in season now."

"I would like to try one, but I didn't bring any money with me this morning."

"You don't need to worry about that," Percy said. He went over to his basket, and, disregarding the first two he touched as not quite perfect, he selected the mango most ripe but still firm and another for himself. I watched him peel back the thick green hide with his teeth, tossing the hide in the trash barrel in the same motion. I did the same, missing the barrel. Pale gold juice ran down over my chin.

"How do you enjoy it--nicely?"

"One of the best things I ever ate."

We exchanged mango smiles.

"How many pounds of roots do you need?" I asked. "You get sixty or seventy at once?"

"Oh, you mean yams. Yes. I would say about seventy or seventy-five pounds."

"Would you say you use about three hundred pounds in a week?" I asked, guessing.

"More than that."

"Yeah? Five hundred pounds?"

"Yes, and can be that or more than that, too. Because remember, you have to buy Mondaytuesdaywednesdaythursdayfridaysaturday. Because tonight--and then it is tomorrow. And sometimes we have to buy from other people too, because food finish. Please excuse me now. I have to be getting soon back. Sylvie, my wife, is alone in the kitchen, and we get very busy, you know. Mount Salem drivers eat at my restaurant. Would you like to see it, and my home, too?"

"I would like to see it," I said. Percy picked up the basket with the mangoes on top and one sackful of yams. I picked up the other sack of yams and we walked out of the market together, into a lifelong friendship.

I was huffing by the time we walked five hundred yards uphill in the hot sun, to where we could stop a cab. "You do this every day?" I asked, between breaths.

"Must. The drivers do not like to go to the market. Too much extra weight."

Several cabs passed before one would stop. We loaded at least a hundred pounds of vegetables in the trunk, then took off up the mountain on a curving road. The cab ran just as fast as the driver could get it to go, speed shifting, motor racing, children, goats, and stringy runt dogs jumping out of the way. The small taxi turned this way and that down streets narrow enough for only one car to pass at a time, the horn blasting around still more curves before coming to a stop alongside an unpainted wooden building with a "Red Stripe" beer sign nailed to the unbleached wood.

Children came up to watch us unload and to stare at the strange white man. We carried the food to the side door of Percy's restaurant. The driver sat down and ordered breakfast. Percy brought it to him. Sylvie was in the kitchen with several gallons of steaming soups and stews. We were introduced, with more smiles all around.

"Have you ever eaten *ackie* and codfish yet?" she asked.

"No," I said. "What is it?"

"It is our national dish. You must try it." She brought out two dishes of what looked like scrambled eggs--lumpy, yellow and soft.

"This is called ackie?" I felt like a tourist.

"Yes," Percy said. "That is the tree of it out in the yard," he added, pointing toward the open door. "My own are not ready as yet. They must burst open and let the poison water run out. And then you can eat them."

I gulped.

In the side yard next to the restaurant, near the ackie tree, stood a man with a dark beard and a soiled red cap, sawing on a carved mahogany headboard. Four curved bedposts leaned against the shed beside him. His curled hair brushed wildly out from beneath his hat. Streaks of white in his hair and beard showed a carpenter at his prime perhaps sliding past middle age. Papa John Hall, the drum builder, was making a bed.

Percy and I ate our breakfast. After green tea he said, "Why don't you sit and rest. I must go cut up cow-foot."

"Mind if I watch?"

"Come then."

We walked out the side door of the restaurant and along the narrow alley between the houses of unpainted bords. All that could be seen were small wooden houses, fences and coconut, ackie, and lime trees scattered around. Clothes hung on lines and stretched between trees. An outside shower made of cinderblocks was next to a sink for washing clothes outside. A well-used washboard stood in a bucket of soapy water where Percy's daughter washed out clothes. Percy's mom bent over a steaming pot of her own, cooking over broken pitchfork prongs resting on three rocks. A chicken ran under the house and three chicks zigzagged frantically after her.

Over a black iron charcoal burner lay two cow's feet, from the knee down. The singeing hair smelled more than a little foul. Percy took up the cow feet one at a time scraping them clean with a knife. He cracked the bone with a machete, bringing the big knife high over his head and down hard. Percy's dog, a little black and white mongrel with a bobbed tail was fatter than the rest of the dogs hanging around. He came close and snatched a small piece of bone that flew toward him.

"Bruno!" Percy said firmly, but he let the dog be. Two skinny wild dogs stood off at a distance, waiting for it to be over so maybe they could sneak just enough to eat to hold their own lean bones together. I could see no meat on them, just countable ribs.

"This is the best part of the cow," Percy said, shoving at the marrow with the tip of the machete. "Builds strength."

"What do you make with them?"

"Cowfoot stew. You must try some of it. I have to help Sylvie now. You could sit on the verandah and rest, if you like."

I didn't feel like resting, so I walked through the narrow alley again, down to the end of the street, past big garbage bins that no one ever seemed to empty. A black and white spotted goat stood on top of the heap, eating a banana peel flipped out of the corner of his mouth like a bright yellow tongue. I saw hogs wallow in murk. Further along I came to a large green meadow, called "the commons," with the mountains behind. Goats moved in herds and cows grazed freely--no fences. Looking down from Mount Salem, bluegreen hills roll toward the bay of deep blue water, lighter near the shoreline, the view blocked by tourist buildings. Looking only inches tall from the heights of Mount Salem, tourist money came before the sea. Not far away, smoke curled upward toward white clouds. The dumps were burning. Black smoke rose.

The sun was beginning to get hot now. Vultures rose into the air from the rocks where they were sunning themselves. I went back to Percy's and found the shade. Palm trees waved like arms in morning breezes. Everything should have been peaceful and quiet, but I got thinking about this half-finished book, *Boskydell Blue*, back home. Would it ever finish? How would it finish? Is it a novel anyway?

A shirtless man of twenty-six or so walked by in front of Percy's verandah. He looked toward me and smiled. His face was pure delight. He wore a finely shaped Ethiopian nose and had a wooden soda crate in one hand. When he is even with where I was sitting, worrying, he put the crate on the ground carefully., like it was made of glass. He walked around it, kind of dancing with the rhythm as he sang to me in a snappy calypso beat, popping his fingers.

"If you got something to do--
Don't let no one
do it better than you."

The man picked up his box and went into a fenced yard across the street. I followed him and in that moment he decided for me to do the best I can. Because no one can tell what I got to saybetter than I. Can they? Can they?

Sambaro, sometimes simply called Barro, lives in one room of a house across the street, on the property where Percy's bakery with its round brick oven is built. Barro works at the tourist clubs as an entertainer. He was tying a rope around the neck of his mama goat, and her twin kids butted under her, lifting her hind feet clear off the ground. He and I got to talking and we smoked together some during the three days we stayed on Mount Salem, because Percy would not allow me to go back and stay at the hotel. We were his guests. Good thing, too, because I was flat broke and so was Mottsy.

Mottsy! By then it was close to noon and I remembered my friend back at the hotel room we had rented for one night, taking most of the money we had. I brought Mottsy up to Percy's and after dinner we all settled down on Percy's verandah, listening to the jukebox blaring reggae music and watching kids kick a soccer ball up and down the street.

In the black sky, between the palm leaves moving in the night air, crisp clear starts shown. The moon was full and Papa, the drum builder, was drunk. He weaved a little, coming up to the verandah. He picked up two pop bottles where the kids had left them and he said loudly, "So, you do not think I can do it then?"

Papa John placed one pop bottle on the edge of Percy's porch and tried to balance the mouth of a second bottle on top of the first, like an hourglass. The top bottle wobbled uncertainly. The porch rail is not parallel to the ground.

"Nah, I don't think so," said I.

"I don't think so either," said Mottsy.

Percy said nothing. He had seen Papa drunk before. Papa balanced one bottle upon the other, slowly removing each finger until his creation stood uneasily for a moment, then tumbled down toward the concrete walkway. Papa reached out and caught the falling bottle in one hand with the same motion, swung it back, and held it still. Top to top---hourglass minus sand and regulated neck.

"SO!" Papa shouted, and jumped away, arms held wide from his body, parallel to the earth, still weaving slightly. The balance held and Papa's face was pure delight. A big man he was, whose unruly white hair streaked his dark and wild beard. Later on that night Mott and I went around to his one room. It had a white enamel basin on a little wooden platform built out from one window. Papa had to lean out the window in the early morning to wash his face. There was a single oil lamp to fill the room with gentle light.

"Thy kingdom come, Thy will be done," Papa said.

"You mean, a prophecy?"

"Yes," Papa said, softly. "At the ends of time, and within time, too."

"What is coming?"

"A new world. People moving with each other with equal feeling and--" Papa's words blurred quietly into each other at the end of his thought and we could not hear them.

"Feeling?"

"Yes. All functioning from that same wholeness and holiness and the oneness of love."

"In my lifetime that's going to happen?" I was incredulous.

"Must happen," Papa said. "God's will be done. That which is destructive going to be removed, you see."

"Destroyed?" Mott sounded concerned.

"Yes, by is own evil. Because man makes what he cannot control. Out of disobedience. Disobedience. They follow their own thoughts. God did not mean the riches of the earth for only a few. But those people don't get very far. They carry a shadow of evil within and around them, you know. The same thing reflects. So the alternative now is to do good, and good will follow you. For what you sow, you shall also reap."

"Sometimes it is hard to know what is good," Mott said.

"You see? Well, it does appear so. Because of the unrevealed condition in every circumstance," Papa said.

"Oho," I said, laughing. "Beware the unrevealed condition! You mean in every circumstance there is an unrev--"

"Yes. Yes, it does appear..."

"Then how can we hope--" Mott began.

"But your faith shall make you whole," Papa said, mumbling the words together, his voice becoming hardly a whisper.

"What?"

"Ffff---" Papa said again, mumbling because he did not have his teeth in. "Your faith shall make you whole and right there now cause things to take the shape which is constructive."

"Oh. Faith. But what about people who have blind faith?" asked Mottsy.

"What do you call blind faith? Faith without the physical eye?"

"Without reason," Mott said.

"Well, there is no faith like that, you know. It would have another name," Papa said.

"What is it called?"

"It should have another name, that condition which you describe. See if you can find another name for it, because faith--*the first seed that can grow a faith tree is patience.*" Papa said this softly.

"Ahh, here we go," said I.

"Is patience," Papa repeated.

"Oh, boy."

"Endurance. Perseverance, and all those other joys. Patience to make faith. See? So unless those is used thoroughly den, you can't get the other word of the world, yunnerstand, the glorified word. Those are the ones that suffer and come through great tribulation by these testings, these conditions that become adverse to his thinking and way of living, yunnerstand. Those are come as obstacles for him to overcome and surmount, for He is a living God, that dwelleth--"

"You mean each man is a living God?" I interrupted.

"Yes the living God dwelleth within. And he doesn't keep anything from the man that the man would desire."

"What if you desire a sailboat?" Mott asked.

"Whatever you desire, but it might not be working towards the good of humanity. Might belonging more to Caesar's world. Just the physical world."

"How about those who have things that are not developed for the good of humanity, like the bomb?"

"You mean the bombs that men develop? They have only been developed through carnality," Papa said.

"I thought you were saying that man only gets what is basically good."

"No, he gets what is evil, but what-- He gives it, but he is not happy to get it. No one is. No one."

"Mmmmm."

"He gives it without a second thought. Don't he? That outer and that inner must come in oneness. Whatever is done in the night can be meeted in tomorrow in the statement or in the action again. Yunnerstand. And that holiness now just carry it on eternally in rightness, have it register in goodness and will litter seeds around of faithfulness and all sorts of glorious conditions that represents constructiveness constantly. Beams of light beaming in whatever those ways that you constantly practice and believe, yunnerstand. After a while you will be filled--those seeds will be able to bear fruit and make your judgement become different from the others who--"

"What are the seeds again," I said. "Patience and what? There were three or four of them."

"Patience is one. Long suffering would be another. Yes. Endurance. Yes. All those are just patience, sister and brother. They all suggest a way. Even when my mother was dying, I saw her in a condition of *discrimenin* spiritually and physically away. I figured that she wanted something spiritually--a thought spiritual, you know? And I ask her and she said yes. I took the Bible up and open it and read the twenty-seventh psalm, that said the Lord is light and salvation, of whom shall I fear, the Lord is the strength of my life, of whom I should be afraid. You know?" Papa again spoke so gently we could barely hear him.

"And that can be of an affirmation. In a moment when the heart fears, or thought--weakness within the soul. Yunnerstand. You just rise up in that and within that and--" Papa John took in a great breath of air through his nostrils, chest rising. The light from the kerosene lamp caught and flashed his left eye, while all around his head his dark hair curled a wild halo. "You make life again as the creator once did. Yunnerstand."

"Mmmmm."

"Becoming a living soul again," he mumbled.

"What?"

"And become a living soul, although you were yet dead within a moment, both in thought and feeling. You see, affirmation is the only conscious way of having the soul coming on the crossroad or turning around to do better. The sword that can constantly fight the enemy away. And builds a unity. Unified force." Dogs began to howl at the night and then at each other. Papa continued. "The affirmation, because it strengthen your exactive power. Your will, and everything. Yunnerstand. After you goes on for a while, sometimes you come to some circumstances where you need external help or internal, you know?"

"Mmmmm."

"You just hear the spirit rise up within! 'I am the Lord thy God who brought thee out of the hand of bondage, thee shall have no other God before me!' At night you are somewhere alone and you hear something unusual. You just turn unto another thing again, just like in the twenty-third psalm-- 'I fear no evil for thou art with me.' Constantly affirm His presence again! Unify yourself to a--" and the end of his sentence faded off. Dogs barked in the night.

"Evil is not to be feared," I said, "But do you think it should be fought?"

"Evil? Yes, it should be constantly, because it is stronger, you know. Evil can fight good, but only it can fight it, what you would say, fifty percent. Yunnerstand."

"Fifty percent?"

"Yes, that is like the champion of evil has fifty percent endurance of the champion of good. Yunnerstand."

"Why don't they both wrastle it out, good and evil, and leave mankind alone?" I asked.

"Well, you see, good and evil in *Isea* forty-three, one God say he made them all and He said He made-- All things were made by Him and without him weren't nothing made that is made. So all things that is made by him--those little roaches you see running off and getting terrified of--were made by Him and must be. All these are plagues."

"You know what he said earlier?" I said to Mott. "There was a three inch roach in the back room. Eeeow, it was flying around and bouncing off the walls and running up my back. Papa said it was a super roach because it was eating off those spiritual books he has under his bed." All three of us laughed at that.

"I'm going to bed," Mott said.

"He said that," Papa said, laughing, looking at me.

"He said that," I said.

Standing up, Mottsy said, "Many people call it different things, but it's all the same teaching."

"Sure," Papa said, with conviction. "Naturally. Well, He promised to make those things strengthened and over the earth as how the water cover the sea. Equally as how you see the water never become unequaled in level condition--unless it's rough. It's tempestuous. You can see it's looking level all of the time." He motioned toward the Caribbean Sea with his brown arm. I imagined the sea rolling up easily onto the white sand, a mile down the hill called Mount Salem.

"He promised that righteousness will be equal to that, you know. Yes. By men thinking one way into goodness and trueness-- by seeing that he makes good and he makes evil, you have to have a moderated understanding within the judgement of these forces. Cause He made them both, you know. one God. some people think the devil is an extra power, but He's *alladevilandgodinone*."

"In man?" Mottsy asked.

"Yes. And whether man does good to one another or evil, is the God or Devil in him," said I.

"That's the manifestation of a God, too."

"Yeah?"

"Into His ways of development because take it in a superiority, take it for a superior being. He becomes creative and made all things. There were nothing functioning without His source and force. Yunnerstand. So you must include Him in all functions. Ha ha ha. He has some temporary standing in some and some eternal standing in others. But they all make a development. They all make a way towards the end."

"Mmmmm." I was starting to space.

"Because by knowing good--by knowing bad you realize good, you know," Papa said.

I repeated to make sure I understood. Or at least heard correctly. "By knowing bad you realize good?"

"Yes. You are taught good. Because when the bad reach you, you always know there are an opposite. That which you have experienced in the beginning or before which weren't what you experienced. Yunnerstand."

"Mmmmm."

"Yes. That is why man become so satisfied within himself when he is innocent to any accusations. Yunnerstand And that is wy he becomes so distressed in himself although he pretends that he is not guilty, and he is guilty. He has an inner conviction for himself at that time. He cannot sleep that thought out at all, by no condition. Only condition that can sleep that condition out of him is death. Put a rope to his neck, a pistol to his ear. Which is the utter destruction of his physical, his mental, his spiritual--mmm out, out of his life."

Wild dogs howled in the dark.

"So those confused stages that take man and cause him to take suicide of himself. At times no savior, no counselor to give him a suggestion which is the higher kingdom. Take him on a higher plane."

"I don't quite agree," said Mottsy, who had not gone to bed after all. "Always he's having to feel guilty."

"Well, he feels guilty when he is wrong," Papa said.

"Right. Whenever he is wrong, but he doesn't have to feel wrong," Mott said. "He has a choice of feeding wrong or feeding right."

"Oh, not like that! You must never think that," Papa said.

"Why not?" Mottsy asked.

"Because that's what he sows he has to reap. Equally to what his sowing reflects. That always equally."

"You always get repaid," said Mottsy.

"From what you do," Papa completed the thought.

"If you go about doing right you will be paid far more than what your actions--"

"Yes," Papa John said. "Well you are supposed to be paid back ten times if you do right.

"Such a bargain!" I mocked. "The world should hear of this."

"You don't believe it, though," Mottsy said.

"Sure I do," I said, laughing. "What was it you were saying? That when the police sees a Rastaman--"

"Yes. So long as he sees a Rastaman he sees a herb tree," said Papa.

"Someone told me there are not many Rastas arrested."

"Yes. You see, He promised to keep away these pestilence and things away from the righteous. Yes, but He also suggests that you should watch. Yes. And you should pray. You should also use your eyes to the fullest extent, and your *wisman,* which is wisdom within man, and the ways you understand to be wiser than the serpent and more gentle than the dove. *For when you do your best, the Father does the rest."*

It sounded like a bumper sticker line to me, and Papa's two sons, Melvin and Blooks had slept through all this reasoning on the one double bed Papa also slept on. One room lit, soft oil lamplight, "Home Sweet home" on the mantel.

ACCORDING TO JOHN THE CARPENTER

What is coming?
A new world. People moving with each other with equal feeling, all functioning from that same wholeness and holiness and the Oneness of love. That which is destructive is going to be removed. So the alternative, the affirmative now is to do good, and good will follow you.
Sometimes it is hard to know what is good.
Well, it does appear so, because of the unrevealed condition in every circumstance. But your faith shall make you whole. These conditions that become adverse to his thinking and way of living, yunnerstand, those are come as obstacles for him to overcome and surmount, for He is a living God, that dwelleth within, and He doesn't keep anything from the man that he would desire.
What if you want a sailboat?
Whatever you desire, but it might not be working toward the good of humanity, might belonging more to Caesar's world, the physical world. That outer and that inner now must come in Oneness, yunnerstand. And that Holiness now just carry it on eternally in rightness, have it register in goodness, and it will litter seeds around of Faithfulness and all sorts of glorious conditions that represents constructiveness constantly--beams of light in those ways that you constantly practice and believe, yunnerstand, and after awhile you will be filled, those seeds will be able to bear fruit and make your judgement become different from to others.

RASTAMAN AT THE UNIVERSITY

    Before the fate of the rockfest had been settled, a little brown man wearing a red sly hat stepped off the Greyhound bus in Carbondale. Percival Lester Thompson III looked much smaller than I remembered, but he shook my hand just as hard. I took Percy's bag from him, put it in the bed of the pickup, and drove six miles south of town to the farm.

    Percy met some friends while visiting from Jamaica, and he was invited by Chuck Pettis to be a guest lecturer at one of Bucky Fuller's design classes at Southern Illinois University. Inside the big ultra-modern classroom, plastic formica fake-wood tiers of tables circled around the center of the room in rising layers, like a tiny arena. Unseen men stood ready by their machines in the audio control room and Percy stood small and alone in the center of the stage.

The class clapped and the little man with a piece of carved root sticking out of his pocket smiled and waited, patient and at ease, until the applause finished.

Silence.

"Ladies and gentlemen, brothers and sisters. I greet you under the auspices of One Love, one unified love. Divided-- we fall. United-- we stand. These sounds would you say with me please? 'May the words of my mouth and the meditation of my heart be acceptable in Thy sight, oh Jah, my strength and my redeemer who liveth and reigneth over all human *etherience*!'"

The little Rastaman was silent then, walking before us, looking into the young faces turned toward him. "Could you please regard the color of the skin of a man." He held out a black arm for us all to see. "God created man from nature, and no one univershall group have no *prehemiency* over the *impignation* of skin because it is what nature provides what we eat, and also produces the beautiful *materialize* of our bodies, and the system of man... and produces his vision.

"Why do we live among each others as you'd call it the lower animals? Do you realize and know that the animals of the earth behave themselves more better than man do, and likewise... and men do likewise as some of those lower animals do also. But I know man was created after nature. In the beginning was God, and the word was with God and the word was God take on flesh!

"Where it dwells?" Percy asked proudly. "Where do the word dwells when a man speakest? Could you please tell me, my brothers and sisters where the word dwells? Can you see it? Yes or no, in English."

Percy walked before us, looking at all our blank faces, still waiting for an answer. We looked around the room, not knowing what to think.

"I do want this article," Percy continued. He pointed to a pencil on the desk. "I repeat the word first. The sound is gone. Who goes materially and fetch this article? Bodily I go and fetch this article." Percy walked over and picked up the pencil from the desk.

"Good and bad. Negative and positive! When I'm speaking, I speak *univershally.* And this is an undefeated genealogy! You could be a monthly *prognegater,* stargazer, scientist-technology.

Simple coming from nature. Art! Science! Art! What is science? I mean, uh, can anyone answer what the term science is? Could you please, I speak among you, my brothers and sisters?

"Can anyone explain to me what is science? I would really like to know your true knowledge. Man got his knowledge from the animals what is on the earth. I remember going to school and my school days. Men learn their science from the animals that feeds on the herbs of the earth, because you watch the animal and he ate it, and he doesn't go staggering, neither do he go drunken. He survives because he ate it to get sustenance, strength to keep the life in the body.

"Why should we learn hate-- and do not learn love? Love and hate. Why hate?" he asked softly, quietly, gently. "Why not love one another, brothers and sisters of one noble united nation, *Univershally*?"

Percy waved his arm around the four corners of creation. "I mean when I speak, I love you as I love myself. I'm not responsible for the *impignation* of my skin-- that is nature. Learn that we are on an ere now. Which I greet you under the auspices this way, 'SALA MANA KATA, HEEDA HEEDA WADDADA.' When I say to you in *Swaheylie* language, that is *Hammeric* tongue.

"Oh I greet you, brothers and sisters. Let us all live together and unite. Only one thing rules freedom, the people will not unite. Brother Alex, that dear brother of mine, that-- oh blessed day when we met each other in Jamaica. Oh beautiful. We shook hands, you know, and I love him. Excuse me when I'm saying I don't mean in a masculine way, or in a feminine way, but when I say I love him, I love him as a brother. What is the image of God? Could any of you answer me that question?"

Since none of us even attempted to answer and fill up the awkward silence, Percy answered it himself. "<u>Man</u> is the image of God. And God is the image of man. When I see you I see God. Oh."

The air left his lungs like a sigh. "Beautiful. God is not a spirit, but the spirit I do speak, but the word that I do speak is spirit, and no man can hold on to spirit. That's the word gone forth. The word dwell in the outermost parts that keeps the life a-going, keep the foot a-moving, *scarve* and hold your gun and go to war... Over what? God is Love. Love the other person as how you love your perfect self. That's love. Do unto him as he have done to you. Love."

Percy looked out among us, waiting to collect some more thoughts. "I came and see brother Alex, spend two months vacation with him. I'm glad the day I met him in Jamaica, and we speak to each others, and we understand each other, and it was a joy because when I saw him he could be a rough man to me. We speak to each others and we understand when you see me coming on a street you being scared of seeing me, what happen? It is nature bring man. This is the way nature produce this skin. This--" and percy grabbed his woolly head, "-- is the way nature give this hair.

"And that is the way nature *revolutes* and brings. What we want to go to war over" WHADEHELLYOUGODOWAROVER?" he shouted. "Like the lower animals. We are not the lower animals." Percy's voice became quiet and confidential. "We are the higher animals. And we have the new version now. There is a catastrophe! We are at the crossroads of the new generation!" Some of the class applauded this line. "Be careful," Percy said.

"The youth... Instead of the older parents teach the youth, the youth got to teach the older parents! The youth got to teach the older parents!" Percy's voice became a little louder, and more applause came. "This is a time of free persons, and when a man, when a person-- If he becomes fifteen years old and him feel him grow his hair and live-- and enjoy the life that you would love, because God is Love.

"The hair upon your head is the glory of God. Oh *beautyfull* queens and kings with their hairs upon their heads-- glorify God-- Because your hair is the covering for your head so that your moral faculties can penetrate the right way. Because your hair keeps your moral cool!"

Some of the longhaired design students laughed loudly. And most of us applauded loudly and furiously. Then we all quieted down and waited.

Silence.

Every eye was on Percy. Nobody was fooling with clothes or toying with pencils. Everyone was looking at the Rastaman.

Percy stood patiently. He was sweating. Serious. Then Percy reached into his baggy coat pocket and pulled out a piece of wood, round and polished smooth white on one end in the form of a pipe. The other end was dark and rough bark, cut out from a tree root the day before when we were carrying roots out of the freshly plowed bottom. Percy held it right out in front of him, moved it from right to left. "I will now turn unto you and show you this article." The class applauded again.

"My culture teach me this! I know I smoke a pipe. I'm going to need one of it. I leave my pipe in Jamaica. I come up here. I feel I would need a pipe. I build a pipe. My skin-- my culture. This is a *scarving* of a pipe. It may not be so refine like your own built. I cut it out with a grass knife. With a pen knife. It is not completed as yet.

"In the older people or the older parents, in their day-- Now is a new generation because the older people harder to understand the principles of the younger generation. And the older people forget to know that this is the twentieth century! This is the twentieth century of the new generation. And the new generation needs to be loving. Needs places to live unmolested. Oh, how happy it would be.

"Could you please tell me-- what power do men have over nature? When I speak, I say that nature revolves or evolves in many forms. The grass that grow is nature. The hair that grow upon your head is nature. What <u>*prehemiency* has man over nature?</u> What the hell, the other man hates the other man because he wears his long hair-- or kept his beard-- he is a coward-- why?

"I feel when I was small and used to read my books I used to see-- when the hunters used to go out and hunt, they hunt the animals that can not be tamed and when they can not get them they shoot them."

"Is that a prophecy?" someone asked.

"Yes," Percy said loudly. "Prophecy!"

The class laughed, and I didn't know what to think. There was another long silence. Then Percy said, "Is there any questions to ask? I'm a so-delighted visitor. Is there any desirous of asking any questions pertaining to nature or science? Plants and so on?"

More silence. "Then what two thoughts were man created with? Man were created of two thoughts-- good and evil. Either do bad. Or do good. One is negative. One is positive. Positive is bad. Negative is good. Everything that is good is God." Percy paused. "Because God is good." Percy laughed. "There is no man on the earth *prittyer* than the other one. Nature. They are in their different forms. Nature.

"All we got to do is love one another, do good unto one another. Do not abuse one another the likes of monies and luxuries. Those are the vexation of spirit. Vanity and Vexation of spirit when I have lots of clothes and boast over it too, and have properties and boast over it, when my brothers and sisters need places to live.

"I don't mean me individually-- I have places to live. I'm an Afro-Jamaican, see what I mean? But we want the younger generation to be united. And the older parents, they fuss about the new generation. The sing the song daily-- Oh, uh, what the song again they sing, Mr. Alex?"

"Teach the children," I said.

"Oh, teach the children well? That's right. And the other part of the matter, they got a dream something of that sort. That song please listen directly-- the moral of that song, those songs they sing about the, uh, father's--"

"Father's hell will slowly go by," I reminded him.

"Go by. That's right. I ask you to write it and give me because that song carry a deep meanings in it. It carry a great moral. Even the songs these youths sings now-- all these youths that sings these songs-- you don't need no weapons to fight a war. Over what? For what you gonna use war weapons for? Over what? What do we live for? Who will be the victor when every man is gone. You tell me who will be the victor. Ha ha ha-- it's so funny.

"Let us all unite and live together as brothers and sisters. Be in fear over any thing. The word fear is not to be afraid. Do not be afraid of a person. Why you being afraid of a person? You must know criminal, you must know *bagabond*, because their ways is crooked. Tells you lies.

"When I speak-- I speak dominant! I <u>love</u> you people, my brothers and sisters. So why not unite? Why not unite with one another? The younger generation time has come! Because we cannot follow the older system. And if this generation, the younger generation follow the older system, it will destroy the youth." Percy's voice grew quiet. "It will destroy the youth. This is the days of the youth because it is a new creation. This is the twentieth century. Kingdom rise and kingdom fall, this is the twentieth century! This is the time of the new generation that sings over your own air, love! Don't it, in the song, please?" Percy looked at me. "Love is coming?"

"To us all." I completed the line for him.

"Love is coming to us all? Oh-- ha ha! It's a joy. Oh, it gives me great impetus! Oh, splendid. Oh I enjoy it-- nicely-- Oh, beautiful. Well, I would say then is there anyone to say anything more or to ask any further questions?"

A girl in the last row said something about her brother going to Vietnam, how he thought he was doing the right thing for his country. "Who is right?" she asked.

"What are they fighting for?" Percy asked back. "I would like to know the true meaning. What are they fighting over?"

A serious young man said, "The world is becoming overpopulated, resulting in certain social difficulties. And I would say we have two alternatives. Birth control or death control."

"Oh," Percy answered. "Let I tell you something. Can I say something to you toward what you say overpopulated?"

"Certainly," said the serious one.

"Oh, yes. Tell me something. Do you know that there is-- uh, infinite that dwell in God?"

"No, I don't," he said.

"Ueh." Percy said. "Would God-- would God created man on the earth and the earth was--mmm-- before man came on the earth was the earth abideth-- therefore, man are not too much on the earth to live! Man are making too much weapons, very dangerous weapons to destroy them own selves through the-- the-- their knowledge!"

"In the total history of the earth war is like the cut of a fingernail," answered the kid. "When you think of the overall benefits of mankind-- we could survive if it weren't for wars. But what kind of life would it be? But the quality of our survival, the nature of our survival, if we-- the overpopulation--"

"Is it right to kill?" Percy demanded.

"Well, uh, but if we didn't limit--"

"Conjunction! You see that word is a conjunction. Is it right to kill? Give me a positive answer!"

"Is a knife right or wrong?" the kid said. "Ever since man's existence he has fought one another. Is a knife right or wrong? The knife is a product of our environment. Man is also a product of his environment. Is man totally right or totally wrong?"

"Did the man made before the knife, or the knife made before the man?" Percy asked. At that the class laughed and began to clap loudly.

"The knife before the man," the kid said uncertainly.

"Well, oh--" Percy said. There were several disgruntled grumbles by the class. "And the man behind the knife? Who made the knife?"

"What do you consider a knife? Before the knife was a sharpened stick." The kid was trying to wriggle off the hook.

"No!" Percy said firmly. "He who live by the sword shall perish with the sword. Because he is certain of his sword and he-- he-- he's uncertain the other way. Ha ha ha." The class laughed loudly, each person looking to each, and through the applause Percy continued. "You see, man's heart thinks of war. Man's heart thinks of peace because when he makes war, war is hell, and he's afraid of it too! Ha ha. That's Satanic power! That the man who develop evil in terms of Satan. See what I mean. That's my sentiments. How would you terms that? Is there any meanings behind that? What would you say?"

"That's your own views," the kid said.

"No. Think it wisely! That's not my own views. I speak internationally. I speak *univershally.*"

The class laughed. "Well," said the kid, "There are those who disagree with you."

"No," Percy said in the tiniest voice possible, like some people talk to kittens.

"There are <u>not</u> people who differ with you?" The kid sounded amazed.

"Do you love me?" Percy gently asked.

"Certainly people going to war--"

"Do you love me as your self? Do you love me?"

"Yes," the cynic quietly said.

"As you love yourself?"

"Yes," he said, more quietly still.
"Would you do unto me as you would do unto your self?"
"Yes."
"Well, that would change your heart," Percy said, as we all warmed up in generous laughter. Even the kid.
"Evil comes from man's heart. No other source. There is good and bad there. You must exorcise them. The right way." There was a pause and everyone sat in silence for awhile. "Is there any more questions?" Percy asked.
"How, with the world as complex as it is--"
"Remember when you ask a question. When I am speaking, remember that this is globally. Internationally. This is from one globe from one corner of the world to the other corner. It affect all nations. The younger generation. They want to be free. Free choice. Free choice. Think freely. Think an easier way of life how to live. <u>Too much economic pressure is on man.</u> Those are the things that is on man. While other things move-- go and build other materials which have no use to man other than destroy them living soul. Man is a living soul and he must live for a purpose. Want to live and enjoy-- oh-- all of us sitting here and enjoying the atmosphere. Free to breathe it. How happy we are. We are not stifled. Not living dead people. We are <u>live</u> people. Oh beautiful.
"Would it is nice to see us sits around the table communicating with each other. Brothers and sisters. In a peaceful coexistence. Regardless of no look whatsoever, or no color of the skin of a man. He is not responsible. Nature. Nature is responsible. So if you can find nature, look for him. Ha ha ha, because nature is a revolution and revolution means revelation and revelation means what? Rebels and *rebells*. Hear me rebels!
"These are the ages which Moses lead the people of Israel out of the land of bondage, take them back to the land of *Canna*! They ask him various questions as you likewise get them present day now. And they say unto him, um, um uh, well, the people say they are not going, and Moses say unto them, 'Here me rebels!' What the terms revelation means, uh, you're, uh, you genius or genealogists, what is it meant? Please. The word reveals in revelation. I mean I would like to know the answer. You could look inside your encyclopedia, Webster's dictionary, and you'd find that word you see there, and tell me the meaning if I am

telling you a lie. I want every man to understand what I'm saying because I do speak plain English."

"How about herbs?" someone asked.

"The Bible says within herbs is the healing of the nation. Just as the herbs of God keep the earth cool-- if the grass is cut from the earth, or cut by a machine, and cleaned from the surface of the earth, what kind of result do you get from that purpose when the sun does penetrate through?"

"Burns up," said a student.

"It dry," Percy agreed, "Because the substance have been wasted. After the grass is on the earth and cover the earth, when you turn over the soil, oh, <u>enrichen</u>. It enrichen, because the hair-- the grass is the covering for the earth just as how the trees got their branches and leaves, oh beautiful they are in the sight of beauty. And what is man? Man evolve for a purpose. Man did live for a future. What is future? Culturally speaking. Because this is a new era." Percy's voice took on a tone of humility. "This is the age of a new generation and it must take its stand. In one unified love. One Divine love. *Univershally.* Internationally. Whether you want to be an Indian, whether you want to be a *Chinee* man, whether you want to be a yellow man, whether you want to be an African, it <u>must</u> be."

*****

Percy's lecture on peace was recorded and was sent to the woman's brother in Vietnam. He went AWOL, left the war and the killing, and flew away to Jamaica to meet and reason with Percy. A Jamaican baker spoke words powerful enough to bring a young American soldier safely home from war. Early, too.

Photograph by Larry Jasud

LOVE IN THE COCKPITS

Only the tallest mountain tops show up blue where the shadows hold them, changing to deep green when the sunlight reaches. Bongo Adolphus walks by with his machete in his hand, chanting, "Rasta chanting on-a Mount Zi-on-I!"

"Love up!" he hollered as he walked down the road.

"Love Rasta!" I shouted back to him. I was sitting in the doorway of the unpainted little house. It had three rooms and each room had a door opening to the outside. If you look out the door facing east, limestone rock bluffs rise straight up the hill covered with green vines and wide and shiny-leaved plants. Crawling snake-like cactus look succulent without spikes. Behind the little gray house, five or six breadfruit trees have wide deep green leaves as big around as arms can reach. The fruit is like green softballs, swelling even larger, until ready to roast. It tastes like fresh baked muffins, or, when boiled in soups, like artichoke hearts. Lots of them.

The door facing north frames banana, banana, and more banana trees like huge grass plants. Blades rise up out of the center out of a rain. A rolled up single leaf like a scroll or map often grows tall as a man, and then slowly unrolls in the sun. Hummingbirds sip nectar from the rose-colored banana flowers, hanging still in the air as if suspended by an invisible wire, wings simply a blur around them. I had green banana porridge with fresh grated nutmeg. Country ladies would come up to the house, delighting to show me how to cook Jamaican. I had ripe banana fritters fried up crisp and sweet, and roasted plantain cooked over an open fire.

The front porch faces south where two streams meet at the old wooden footbridge, one forked from Bongo Adolphus' yard, and the other spring not fifty steps from the house, spilling over the rocks. I washed clothes ankle deep in running spring water, had fresh water for drinking and tea coming directly from the earth, and tumbling farther on down the hill in gentle murmurs.

One day about a quarter to noon I was walking along the path that finally winds around to Adolphus' cultivation and I heard a lot of water falling. I followed the sound and came to a place where the stream had cut a deep ravine in the side of a hill, falling fifteen feet or so onto a rock ledge. Ferns and mosses grew between and over the rocks.

I climbed down the steep bank thinking it would be easier coming back up. In a short time drops flew from my hair and back, catching rainbows in the sun. It was February. Drying off, I walked along the stream where it curved away from sight into the green leaves. There was a huge bunch of green bananas that had grown so heavy it had fallen into the creek area. Two fingers had begun to rot, while most of the hands were swelled and full, ready to ripen. They must have weighed over thirty pounds.

I stumbled up the creek, slipping barefoot over rocks, taking my time. When I got back to where my clean clothes lay spread out to dry on bushes, I was sweaty again. I stepped, splashing, under the falling water, looking up the nearly vertical hill of loose dirt. Good practice, I thought.

The truth is that it is easier to climb up a hill when footing is bad if you have a big bunch of bananas on your head, because the additional weight, if shifted correctly, becomes help rather than a burden.

I walked back up the hill refreshed. the sun was not yet too hot for comfort. I gathered some banana trash--banana leaves dry out and droop down along the stalk, or trunk. I hung the bananas on a rope after wrapping lots of banana trash around them. "To help them ripen quicker," Mr. Graham's son Huntly had said.

I was just getting the knack and fun of country living--opening coconuts, climbing for breadfruits, digging yams while being careful not to "juke" them with the tip of the machete. walking down the path toward the wooden footbridge I saw a small, bearded white man wearing a polka dot sly hat. A woman and baby child were with him.

It was the end of winter and the last time I had seen old Mottsy was last fall. Joannie had little Rachel slung over one hip and a whole covey of brown Jamaican kids following, laughing and playing. They looked like a parade with Mott in the lead. Rachel was all laughing and hollering as the kids touched her gently to see if she was real or whether she would break. They probably had never seen a white baby up close before.

I jumped up when I saw my friends and ran down to the wooden footbridge to give them all a big hug. The Jamaican kids hooted and hollered and we were all laughing because I may have been jumping up and down, I was so happy and surprised to see them. More happy than I could ever tell Mottsy in words. And there he was, standing as real as a mango tree.

"What are you doing here?"

"There ain't much growing in old Kentucky, and we got your letter--something about living on a banana farm--so we thought we'd stop and visit for awhile. We're crazy about bananas."

"Well, you come to the right place. You're just in time for some fresh-roasted coffee. man down the road has a tree of it."

Mott and his family spent a week or so eating bananas and one day he and I went down to fetch a piece of dry and yellow bamboo for kindling. We trimmed it off with the machetes we had bought for seventy five cents each. We were dragging thirty foot lengths up the hill toward the house. While we were resting along the path looking out over the wide valley, up the hill toward us, whistling, came Bongo Adolphus, a basket of yams on his head.

"Love up!" he shouted.

"Love Rasta!" I shouted back.

"Hi," Mottsy said quietly.

"You are my brother?" Adolphus asked, looking hard at me.

"Sure," I said.

"And you are *not* my brother!" Adolphus said to Mott, his voice hard and flat.

Mott looked dumbfounded and hurt. "How come I'm not your brother?" he asked.

"You come upon your brother and you can't greet him with love?" Adolphus asked back.

"Love, Man," said Mott.

Adolphus talked some about how he pushed fifty yam sticks in the ground that day, saw me looking at his spliff, and passed it to us. I said thanks and praises to the Most High.

"*Jah, Rastafar I*," he said, setting three yams in the deep grass before us and walking on up the hill. After a while we could hear him whistling his chant again. We watched white birds drifting before distant horizons.

"Pretty intense little guy," Mott said.

"Damned hard worker. That's his farm you see way down in the valley. Yam banks right up the hill. You can see them from here. That reddish brown patch in all the green. He helped me rent the little house. Also helped with food--as you can see," I said, looking at the yams.

"What are those--potatoes?"

"No, yellow yams. We'll have them for supper." We walked back up to the house carrying the bamboo and the fresh-dug yams. Joannie was sitting in the doorway and Rachel was sucking on a bottle.

"The landlord's son," she said, "the oldest one--what's his name?"

"You mean Huntley?"

"Yes. That's the one. He just came up with some fresh cow's milk for Rachel."

After Rachel finished the milk she squirmed around awhile and then stood up in that awkward, half-bowlegged way babies do. She held onto the doorjamb, bent over to pick up a piece of ripe banana, squished it around in her hands, plopped down on her bottom, and crammed it all into her mouth, forgetting to swallow until she choked, spitting half-chewed banana all over herself.

"You gotta leave room for air," I told Rachel in all seriousness. Joan threw away the lump and gave her a smaller piece until she ate all she could hold and lost interest. She got cranky and finally fell asleep.

"Looks like island life appeals to her," I said.

"She's not the only one," Joannie said, smiling lovingly at Mottsy.

ACCORDING TO KINGMAN

So if one would look forward
and throw down the silver,
the gold that dig from the earth,
and turn back to their brothers
they would sight something.
And if they do not want that then--
my Father, His Imperial Majesty
shall cause the foundation of the sea to lay bare,
Him shall cause rocks and mountains
to reel and stagger like a drunken man--
Him shall cause the Heavens
to roll like a scroll and be aparted--
He shall cause this earth
to bomb like a bomball and bustup in flames afire
like a woman's periodical cycle burst in blood.
So leave the Babylonian Colonian Chain
and live the laws of the Almighty God Allahebidon.

Photograph by Larry Jasud

BONGO U

The sand is black along the edge of the bay, curving away from the city in an easy line. The land between the sea and the city dumps is overgrown with green vines and brush. Tin cans, wooden branches, coconut husks, pieces of plastic, and sun-bleached bamboo litter the beach. The prow of a small, brightly-painted boat points out of the bushes, its red, gold, and green stripes aiming at a sea of pale blue. The sea is only darker out beyond the coral reef where the water deepens and the fish are bigger.

Jack and I, two white men, walk along the changing waterline toward the boat. A constant sea curls edges of foam onto the dark sand, sliding back. Toward us walks a black man. His hair heaps around his head in large knotted pieces. He smiles. We greet each other and I ask him about the boat.

"That ship belongs to a doctor," he says.

"With an office uptown?" I asked, motioning toward Montego Bay with my head.

"No, not that kind of doctor. He is a herb doctor."
"Oh. Can he cure people?"
"Bongo U is a very smart man. Cures cancer, too."
"No," I said.
"Yes," he replied. "I know how he did it, also. Put the blood of a pig and the blood of a cow and the blood of a goat into a vessel, and when they formed a cancer, he went out and found those bushes what killed that cancer. An old white woman went to see him not so long ago, and she came away well. He is a very wise man."

Oh, yeah, I thought to myself. What I said was, "I would like to meet this man who is supposed to be so smart."

Beneath white clouds, waves at our feet rattle small shells against each other, like wind in dry leaves. We moved down along the shoreline toward the place where the boat stuck out of the bushes like a small rainbow. When we got close enough to read, we saw painted in bold, black letters across the prow: "Emperor Haile Selassie I." A small man wearing only long pants appeared next to me. I had not seen him walk up.

"Did you want something?" he asked.
"Yes, I met a man down the beach who said there is a wise man who owns this boat. I would like to meet him. His name is Bongo U. Do you know him?"
"Yes! You would like to talk to Bongo U!"

I was taken to talk to Bongo U. He didn't look much like a man who could cure cancer.

No comb, scissor, nor brush had ever touched his head. The full growth of a black man, near thirty, spun out around his head. We moved underneath his cardboard house, overgrown with jungle like Bongo U's head was overgrown with hair. The west side was open to the sea. Several Rastamen sat in benches made of driftwood and scrap wood covered by tin car roof and green vines as a barrier against the tropic sun. Two men held slowly-burning spliffs rolled in white baker bag paper, cone-shaped like funnels as long as pencils, sometimes thick as a carrot when first lit.

"You bring a friend. What is his name?"
"Jack."
"What is your occupation?" Bongo U asked.

"Oh, potter. Sculpture," Jack said. He didn't mention it to Bongo U at the time, but Jack was also a student of yoga.

"*Sculptury*," Bongo U said.

"Yes."

"Who do you serve?"

"Hmmm?" Jack asked.

"Who do you serve as the Almighty?"

"Whoa," Jack said, his breath escaping. "God. The world. Everybody."

"You serve everyone as that infinite power?" Bongo U asked.

"Ohmmm." Jack was thinking.

"Then what about the individual infinity?"

"The individual-- what?"

"Infinity," I said. "Within each consciousness."

"Aah," Jack said, "The consciousness of all is within each one of us."

"But there is an intelligent power, and that intelligent power embedded within each and every one. But that intelligent power is also an individual. So, who do you serve? Do you serve Time or Nature or Space? Because they are three dimensions. Which do you serve?"

"I serve God," Jack said.

"But God is only a title," said Bongo U.

"Time, Space-- they are all parts of God," Jack said. "They're manifestations of Him. But they are not the true essence of Him."

"Oh, not the true essence. But Time created all things."

"I always thought that time was an illusion, myself. Everything is Now."

"Although it have been now, Time is the master of the foundation of every creative things upon creation. Time. Don't it?" said Bongo U.

"I doubt it?" Jack repeated. He had misunderstood Bongo U's words.

"Don't it," I said. "Only because without Time there isn't any creation. Because creation needs time to take place."

"If there was no creation there would be no Time, and if there wasn't Time there would be no creation.."

"Time is only finite, is it not?" Jack asked. "And God is infinite."

"Infinite power is Time," Bongo U explained.

"Infinite what?" asked Jack.

"Infinite power is Time. The present of Time is Nature. And you have the science of Nature, is Space."

"Is what?"

"The science of Nature is Space."

"Oh. Space," Jack said.

"So within that trinity, the God-like quality. But who is that God-like quality imbedded in individually? There is a God-like quality individually that Divine principle. That intelligent being. What is his name?"

"Well, you call him Haile Selassie, as the manifestation," Jack said.

"As the manifestation. He is the foundation. But the only way you could see God as that infinite power will have to be manifested into a *Staunchable* object."

"Live the Nazarene was, two thousand years ago?"

"Truly," Bongo U said. "I and I, the Rasta, know that there will be ransom from every nation. And within their own God-given right, they serve one God. And the one God should be a God of Consciousness."

"Mmmm," Jack said.

"A God of movement. A God in whom you can see actions, thoughts, and deeds."

"Very true," Jack said.

"To fulfill his own desire to know that that individual is God Almighty."

"Do you ever believe that God can come to rest?" Jack asked.

"Yes. God is only a title. And the word God is given to an individual. But the mere word God, that is material. Because the word. And the word forms itself into an object upon this earth. <u>So God in the western hemisphere means money!</u> Means Money within the western hemisphere. The white man's power is Money! Their dominion is Money! Their authority is Money! Their brutality linked with Money. Their war-like dictatorship linked with Money! Money is the root of all evil upon creation and still is an everyday necessity!"

"You have to have money to live," I said to Bongo U.

"Yes, you have to have money to live, but woe to the man that build a store in his heart to contain it-- Shall cut off!"

There was a pause while Jack and I tried to digest what was just said. Bongo U didn't give us much time for digestion. "Tell I something about your divine--"

"Authority?" Jack asked.

"Or concepts," said Bongo U.

"The concepts I follow you have already said," said Jack. "To have word, thought, action, and deed. And that there is an overpowering, infinite consciousness that I'm part of-- that everyone is part of. Everybody's God. But they have to come to realize it. Man has hidden this fact in his ignorance. That's what I believe."

"Is each and every one create it?" asked Bongo U.

"Everyone is equal. Even the man you think is the worst man is but God himself. You must love everybody. Everything is God. But I am not perfect. So I cannot love everyone. I try. I have much to grow," Jack concluded.

" I have the power to love and to hate! To kill and to make alive, for all power is given to I. The wicked blow out the breath of life because he must live to fulfill prophesy for a short time. Nixon, there, is a wicked liar boy. He is a murder! There is a *bolume* of souls upon his head. He is a traitor, also. But within that cosmic still, my Father do liveth within him. His knee must bow and his tongue confess.

"But creation as a whole is within Selassie I," Bongo U continued. "The stone are Selassie bones. All stone upon creation are Selassie I bones. The rivers are streams of blood that flow through I. The sea are I lifeline, man, that all sons and daughters flow from that line, which is a pool of water, which is Nature. I and I know that the sun is the right eye of Selassie I, the moon is the left eye. The stars are the strands of wool upon his head. We know that!"

"Why do the Rasta take Selassie to be the Almighty?" It seemed a reasonable question to Jack.

"Yes!" said Bongo U. "The world on a whole would like to know why the Rasta take his Imperial Majesty, Emperor Selassie I, our divine worship, as the messiah, as the architector and builder of creation. Is because our Father is *Tieman*, which means Time within man, and out of Time he produceth himself Nature, which is a woman, as water to cool Time, and Time and Nature collorate together and bring forth the tranquillity of Space, that is stars!

"So within that, I and I know that I and I was within I and I Father line when he was also architecturing and building the foundation of Earth-- which is woman. I and I was also emptied into the womb of I and I mother, which is Earth, even unto now. One thing is sure-- that all creative beings, all things dormant and conscious was been architect and build by His Imperial Majesty Haile Selassie I *wisman*, for is wisman, knowledge, and understanding. There are only three revolutionary forces upon creation to which all things have been built upon-- Time, Nature, and Space. And that are my Father, which is ether and water? Words sounds and power! Doors are the consciousness of man.

"All those who are filthy and say they are Rasta are filthy more. All those who are unjust and say they are Rasta are unjust more. And those who are *holar*, I and I the chosen of his table, have been exalted within divinity, authority, and power! Because I and I have been furnished with divine authority to overcome the small stumblingblocks to which Babylon have placed within I and I pathway. But behold! The Lord God of Israel strong and mighty to protect I and I have caused I and I to uplift I and I self from the small things of Babylon. And I and I cannot be bribed by empty treasures, cannot be aid by weak ministry, cannot fall victim to insidious smiles. Because things like those will cause one to call his good authority under brutal feet af might. I and I the son which is the Father and the Father which is the son..."

Bongo U interrupted himself to notice me looking at his slowly burning spliff. "Give him a cigar, yea?" Kingman went into the inner chamber of cardboard walls covered with living vines. He brought out a piece of wood the size of a large book, handled smooth around the edges, knifeworn hollow gnawed around the center by constant cutting. The herb itself was wrapped in a cylinder of white paper, a tube eight inches long and two inches wide. Kingman snapped open his ratchet and sliced the herb as if slicing a carrot, seeds, sticks and all. I could hear the sticks crunch as he sliced.

Blending the herb with a little tobacco, Kingman rubbed it between the fingers of his right hand. His black hair lumped away from his head into pieces, some thick as a wrist but longer, and one large piece down past his neck looked like a flat board. The cutting board and blended herb lay on his lap. He put his knife away and tore a piece of paper printed with "Sunrise Bakery," showing a picture of a sun rising with rays. Kingman carefully rolled a cone-shaped spliff. He took his time and made each move consciously, then handed it to me.

"Thank you," I said.

"Do not thank I," he said, "But give thanks and praises unto the most high. Blessed is the man that walketh not in the counsel of the ungodly, nor standeth in the ways of sinners, nor sitteth in the seat of the scornful. But I and I delight is in the law of the Lord God Jah Rastafar I, His Imperial Majesty, and on his delight do I meditate day and night. I and I shall be like a tree that is planted by the rivers of water that yield I fruit in I season. I leaf, which is I locks, also shall not wither. Nor what so ever I and I do shall prosper. The ungodly are not so, they are like the chaff which His Imperial Majesty drive away. Therefore, the sinners could not stand in the congregation of I and I the righteous, nor they could not stand in the full judgment of I and I the dreadlock host-- Love, the holar patriarchs upon the face of this earth. Blessed is thy holy name, oh Jah, Rastafar I. Fire!"

The Rasta men sitting repeated with Kingman the name of Jah. The herb was lit. I drew deeply and exhaled through my nostrils. At my third draw on the spliff Bongo U continued his monologue. "I and I the son which is the Father and the Father which is the son--"

I interrupted. "Do you think that smoking the herb has some kind of purpose or direction?"

"Yes! Because herbs on a whole is Divine meditative. Herbs. Herbs. There are some scientists that claims herbs to be a *psychochopic* drugs. Within herbs its personal self there is a Divine authority that gathered itself within the cranium of man, that show them inspiration of those God-like qualities that germinate Divine consciousness."

"So, you think that herbs and divine consciousness work together?"

"*Aba*! That is right!" Bongo U pointed a finger at the sky. "Herbs. The government on a whare know that herbs is not bad.

But if the people of this country should go and smoke herbs, the government know that there won't be no workers for his country. And automatically all the people would be Rasta. Whether they clean their face or not, or they shave their face or not, or they *dread* it, they will be Rasta. Because the herbs teach them the quality of Divinity. And this is the only substance to which you have to have deep meditation that those dignities shall cause man to uplift the royal structure of Divinity. I and I, the Rasta, did come to call Israel to His culture."

Jack said, "But many young people in my country smoke herbs, and just sit and become like drunken men."

"Is because they fail to give praises unto the Most High!" Bongo U said. "Herbs can bring madness in excess use, without the proper praises. That man Moses. Did you think it was an ordinary burning bush that gave him that inspiration?"

"Then if you claim Selassie as the Almighty, I still want to see the Father," I said.

"The only way you can see the Father is through I and I the son, because no one can enter the Father but through I. Because I are in the Father and the Father is in I.

"I and I, the Rasta, did come to call Israel to their culture. And they, the black people, named Israel. And they, the black people, named Jew. Because Jew is the fourth son of Jacob, which is Judea. The short name of Judea is Jew. I and I know that His Imperial Majesty, Emperor Haile Selassie I did sit as the conquering lion from the tribe of Judea, the elect God and light of this world. He is king of kings and lord of our lord. No one else could ever take that title. Because that was the title that *Je'sus* the Christ did say was going to come within this dispensation to gathered his chosen from the four corners of creation! And there he sit now as a ruling monarch-- the king of kings in Ethiopia, Addis Ababa, and the God and creator of the universe, the architector and builder of Mount Zion, the wise man, the most humble, infinite person can ever behold is His Imperial Majesty, Emperor Haile Selassie I.

"Behold! If I and I fail to take Selassie I as the Almighty, where are the one forty and four thousand sheep-like people that have been sent down through the earth to gather Israel as a light back to the royal land of Ethiopia?

"Hear I and I and bring forth this message to your congregation, that Rasta did come to guide the feet of man, for they are the high dreads. Rasta are not a cheap formality of human commerce to which have come upon this land through mere curiosity. Rasta have been passed through all realities, bitter experience to stand as a Staunchable object-- to represent the Father in purity, love, holiness, and unity. To live a life above the scribes and Pharisees and Sodosees, and the publican. Because they are-- the *Sodosees*-- they are church people. The scribes, them are lying doctor. So they all are so. Within that cosmic I know for I life have to surpass them before I can enter the Kingdom of Zion, just over that hill. Full few people know who Rasta is, because salt and flesh have been their second nature! They unveil the dead and bury it within the abscess of their stomach! And became walking *cymitry* of living dead-spirits, pocket full of stink and corruption and detriment soul! That's heathen out there to whom he underrate Rasta.

"Because Rasta are not sodomites, Rasta not belly killer, Rasta not pussysucker, Rasta are not cockysucker. Rasta are a Staunchable object of the Almighty, in love, purity, and holiness. To which, who else can uplift the royal structure, the royal Divinity of Mount Zion? Who else can stand as alight in this barren land, that Israel can see a light to hold upon?"

By this time the quality of the herb and the sound of the patois blent together. I was glad that I had the tape recorder along, because although I could comprehend only half of his words, I still wanted to understand the words, if not the meaning, of the things this strange man stood for.

A green lizard skipped across the sandy floor and up a wall quickly. A red circle popped from his throat, probably to attract insects. I heard the Caribbean Sea rolling up onto the beach not fifty feet away.

Bongo U began again. "Though Rasta may be beaten out of consciousness and beaten into consciousness, and may be demurred to the damsels of sorrow to which a ray of sun never did descend by Babylon, let them know that Rasta have to bear this tribulation and affliction and reproach. That Babylon, which is the pope, that old Jeesus bwoy, and the queen gal there, *Elizibug*, I and I come to blast them down to the foundation of creation and burst down their bureaucratic offices, that they may not link their imperialistic governments to conquer Israel into slaverism!"

"I thought Rasta stood for Love," Jack said.

"Yes! So if one would look forward, and throw down the silver and the gold that dig from the earth, and turn back to their brothers, they would sight something. And if they do not do that, then, My Father, His Imperial Majesty, shall cause the foundation of the sea to lay bare, Him shall cause rocks and mountains to reel and stagger like a drunken man-- Him shall cause the heavens to roll like a scroll and be aparted-- Him shall cause this earth to bomb like a bomball and bust up in flames afire like a woman's periodical cycle, burst in blood! My Father shall cause also Mount Sinai to rent in two and cause tears to flow done the strength of her face. Because my Father wrath, to see what-- America! England! The whole western hemisphere have done unto my people! They have beaten them out of consciousness, and demurred them souls to a history of white man's culture! The white man's culture is a culture of barrenness! It is a culture to which demurs one's heart to death, and cause one to feel night and day in the abscess of the earth to where travelers went and never returned. White man's culture leads one unto poverty! Who say then, racial discrimination? Art not I. Neither creed, colored, nor race, not I. I are purity, holiness, I-nety, which is unity, and love. They are the cradle of life. Without those you can never have life. And without affection, compassion, and humility you dare not have love, for it can not grow. I and I, the Rasta, are full of love. The government penalize I and I because if they doesn't do that now, we will bring love and the truth to the people. Because Rasta are well equipped with words, sounds, and power to bring forth all nations to him, and show them Selassie I as the Almighty, because Rasta no show himself as God you know. Show Selassie I."

Kingman began talking at this point. "So, if you search the book of books, which is the Bible, you would see that he fulfill the two thousand year *prophasy*. If you go back within Leviticus eighteen and twenty-one and see the laws of I and I even unto now. 'Thou shall not make baldness upon they head nor round the corners of they beard.' Because there is two laws upon this earth. One law is the material law, the other law is the spiritual law. The spiritual law is the law of His Imperial Majesty, the king of kings and lord of lords. The material law is that of Nixon and Elizabeth and all the western hemisphere. So everyone upon the face of the earth, if they would turn their thoughts and <u>live</u> with the essence of love, the essence of purity, and the essence of holiness, then the entire human race would know each other. If they do not do that, then my Father, His Imperial Majesty, Emperor Haile Selassie I, who sit upon that circled throne that no man can *disamolish* from off this earth, he will judge them in the valley of Jehosophat, Gideon of Gideon, because it is true and it is fit. We are right down in the Gideon. So I am asking the entire universe, the human race sitteth upon the universe, to look aright. Seek aright. Leave the Babyloniancolonian chain. And live the laws of the almighty God, Allahibidon the First! Give thanks and praise to the most high Jah! Rastafar I! That sitteth upon the ancient *ceribims*.

"That Edward give Praises unto him and advocate the throne. So if they entire universe would turn their eyes unto Edward, which is King George's son, they would see he bow to His Imperial Majesty, 1930, second of November, and give black Praises unto him. He bow to him and said he would serve the true and living. God. He come home to his father and he told his father. His father resent it, his father paralyzed after that, on his bed. Then Edward abdicate the throne, because he didn't want to fight against black supremacy. So give thanks and give praises to black supremacy now, and let us live in truth and in righteousness upon the face of this earth. Blessed is thy holy name, Jah Rastafar I the First"

I stopped listening and was thinking my own thoughts. I was not used to hearing this type of logic, nor was I able to believe or refute all the proofs and reasonings of these Rastamen. Several times then, Bongo U repeated a question several times before I realized he wanted me to answer.

"You would like to ask some question?" he said.

"Wha--?"

"You would like to ask some question?"

"Oh. Yes. Uh, if you have all the natural growth on your face do you think it effect the consciousness?"

"Yes, it effect it much, because you are a sinner! Numbers Six state whatever time you are a *holar* person the locks of your hair grow, and razor shall not touch the head. And whatever time the locks of hair is upon your head mean dread! You are a Nazarite Nazarene. So for that reason, member say *Je'sus* was the sweet Nazarene because he came from Nazareth. The high priests didn't think anything good could come out of those Nazarenes, dreadlocks upon their heads. They were looking for a king to come down from the clouds."

"All right," I said. "Suppose I'm wearing all my hair locked up, and beard, and am walking down the street in America, and someone says, 'What you got that mess on your head for?'"

"Say, 'Because I art a full man. I am not diluted. Because woman's face clean. Also because Leviticus twenty-one. Because he transgress against Nature and Time.' The only time a man shave him face now is when he subdue himself unto the bureaucratic offices of Colonian chain for money or the demands of woman. That means he also must take part in their society. You mustn't say you are hippies, you must say you are Rasta, because Rasta are the new name for the Almighty that architect and build you! So I and I did know that Rasta from every nation going to call on Selassia, because they have Egypt for the Ransom and Ethiopia and Sheba for I and I. When Righteousness covers this earth like how water cover the sea, going to be a parcel of pure sheep. No different kind going to be there. All sin going to come off of creation! Everyman--"

The tape ran out there. Jack and I sat among Rastamen, all hair and beards and slowly burning spliffs. In walked a man who could have been a Jamaican plumber or mechanic. His hair was short and flecked with gray, his face was clean. He wore a short-sleeved yellow shirt and wide-cuffed pants. In his hand was a plastic travel bag which said "Air Jamaica" in orange letters. In the bag I could see a crescent wrench, pliers, and other tools sticking out through a broken zipper.

"Love," he said.

"Love I," said several Rastamen.

The stranger sat down on a bench to wait. Bongo U got and went behind a bamboo screen into a little room. In a few minutes he motioned to the man, who got up and went in behind the screen. Rastamen continued to roll and burn spliffs, and listened to the reasoning that just happened, played back on the tape recorder.

Bongo U came out and went over to his medicines, his bottles and tubes and distillers, and flasks, and drying herbs. He brought out a soda bottle wrapped neatly in newspaper, with a cork in the top. When he went back into the small room, I could hear him tell the man, "Take one third of this bottle tonight, one third in the morning, and one third at night. When you finish it, return to I. Also, eat no flesh, fish, nor salt with this."

"Thank you, Doctor," the man said. Returning to the larger room, he nodded to the Rastamen. "Love I," he said, gripping his bottle. He left. Bongo U came out of his examining room with a palm full of herb in each hand. He gave one to Kingman and rolled himself a spliff with the other.

"Is it true," Jack asked, "That if there is anything wrong with you, you can go out and take a bush or an herb or something, and find a natural remedy for what it is?"

"Who?" U said.

"You," I said.

"You mean I! Yes! You see, I art the doorkeeper of the balm that is in Gilead. There is a balm in Gilead, where the sons and daughters of Israel must be healed from their infirmities. Those doctors out there with their little piece of what you may called underrated certificate, borrowed diploma, and all those honorable degrees through society-- I against them. I come to arrest the medical association! Because they have taken my people to make an experimental animal. Impair them up too much. Impair my people too much and cut them up like they are animals, by trying to experiment on my people. For instance, all kind of growth, appendicitis, these things must not be cut. Who give any doctor or medico any authority to use knife upon my people! Who give any of them authority to use any instruments, surgical instruments. No matter whether it is minor or it is major. There should be no surgical instruments applied to the human temple! There supposed to be sufficient botanical herbs to cure all diseases upon earth! And no elements or chemicals. Because elements breed bacterias and virus in the human system.

"But who give I the authority? Rastafar I. The king of kings and conquering lion from the tribe of Judea, who break up the chain! Because have break down philistine chain, break also Nebuchadnezzar chain, also Aepos chain, also Caesar's chain.

Break everyone of them down. Broke also Pharaoh's chain, all of them come down and put on the double power to broke, broke, broke, broke them down, smash up and liquidate, and demolish all council of wickedness! Going to exterminate wickedness off of creation! By righteousness. Love, purity, and holiness. Because the wicked have a very short time to germinate and live, but the righteous live over from generation to generation. Must wipe off creation, because salt gone too far into his bone and flesh too deep in his gut. Can't go to Zion. Wickedness must cut off of creation, and a kingdom of love, holiness, and unity shall maintain every action."

Jack said, "There are many young people in my country believe as you do about wickedness and the time to come. There are many in other countries, too. But I have not seen them. That is one of the reasons I came to Jamaica. To see your people and hear what you have to say. There must be unity between all good."

"The people who are in America are Americans," said Bongo U. "If they should defend America in this Divinity, they also will crash, because America must crash. Because it is a new world now!"

"I cannot believe that," Jack said. "There is no line around America. The world is all one. When peace and love comes to the world there can't be an America and a Jamaica-- they're all one. They will all be ruled by God. When the time comes, they won't defend America, because most of them hate what America stands for. Hate the injustice and wickedness. Want peace and love."

"When you stand for peace and love in a country of wickedness-- There is the most well-equipped police force the world has ever seen, with all kinds of equipment and paid informers, and if you take up the herb--"

"They can't really hurt you if you have peace and love in your heart," Jack said. "Because that peace follows wherever you are."

Said Bongo U, "If you live with peace and unity, love-- holiness and purity are not of the western world, are not of this earth. They are of the throne of Divinity. They have the authority to draw his chair beside the *centairy* sanctuary of holiness, and to reason with love and unity. Which is Selassie I. If one should go into America and defend these things, then automatically that God-like consciousness that resurrect that Divine meditation will move him in time. Because ships from Ethiopia shall flow the western hemisphere and gather each and every one who ever will, may go. Who ever want to live will go. Who want be dead stay in America. Fire burn America, y'unno."

"Burn the wicked, Rastafar I!" said one of the sitting men. "Fireball!" said another, and, "Burn him!"

"I and I know that all the head of state department, all colonial and Imperialistic offices do hate the administration of Theocracy, because Theocracy come to unveil their nakedness. They know that Rasta not speak violence, Rasta no thief, Rasta no beggar, Rasta no drunkard. Rasta is a unique people that come upon creation, that each and every eye shall behold Rasta when him pass, and speaketh either evil or love towards Rasta. Must have to say something.

"Because he see something that he never see before. Because the only way you see man like I and I, it must be the closing of the two thousand year dispensation. That is the only time Rasta come upon action of scenery, is whatever time the closing of a new dispensation is about to lock. And then the reincarnation of the new world come. Then you see Rasta no longer. Any time Rasta lock the door of the old dispensation and open the door of the new reincarnation.

"I and I know who I and I are. The same Peter, James, and John. Elijah, the same Moses, Jeremiah, Isaiah are I and I, the same prophets that come in this land now to gathered all. I and I, the sheep-like people that have been sent down through creation, one-forty and four thousand, the Churchgodhouse of Zion, I and I are saints. Some are high dreads, are angels that come to guide the feet of man. There three stage of man upon creation-- only three. One you call men who clean them face, you have one called man who comb them head, comb them beard and trim it, and one you call Angel, that is I, the sheep-like people that all power and dominion have been given unto, all authority have been passed through I, because we are forty and four thousand, that have been secured from the ways of Babylon. And out of those one-forty and four thousand, I marvel much, for I have seen seven thousand that have heard the voice of him that sit upon the throne as kings of kings and lord of lords, Emperor Haile Selassie I. Say these are my personal structure. They are the seven spirits that go forth unto creation. They are the seven candlesticks to which all light have been gathered from. Those seven thousand cannot be deceived by no one upon creation. I and I are within that seven thousand."

"How many Rasta are there in Jamaica?" I asked.

"Approximately?" said Bongo U.

"Yes."

"Half million, because you have more clean face Rasta than you have natural Rasta. The flags that Rasta wear upon his crown, on his head, are the signification of authority, power and dominion. The rainbow circle. And the rainbow circle that Rasta wear, that is purity, love, holiness, and Unity. I and I, to whom--"

"What do the colors signify?" Jack asked.

"The red is for my blood, flames afire for the wicked. The gold is for my crown, the green for my pastures, my lands, and the Black is for I personal self. That means to say all things upon creation was black before it change. Because when the earth was without void or form, it was in pure darkness. Darkness is blackness. Out of that darkness produce a light. Out of black produce light. So black is the foundation."

Bongo Sherer added, "And the glorification of Zion."

Bongo U went on. "You see, all nations come out of black. So within that cosmic, the virus of colonianism, and the bacteria of imperialism infiltrate the heart and the heavens of black people, and they fall victim to white man's culture and economic bondage."

"Trampled under the brutal feet of might!" added Sherer.

"But careless Ethiopian must go down with go down with Babylon. The one them that take part with Babylon must go down with them, like I take part with Selassie I. <u>The first resurrection sound, I rises first.</u>

"That is why the people are afraid of Rasta. They afraid of Rasta because they are wicked. Because the heart that is perfect cast away all fear. So if the heart is perfect they wouldn't fear them. Good. Because they are the same ones who push a sword into Je'sus side two thousand years ago, when Selassie I come in that form. After Je'sus give them fish and bread. They are the same one that stone Moses in the wilderness after Moses open the four wings of heaven and call out feather, fowl, and hog, because they lust after it. Come back this time as backlash and weapons. One thing is sure-- Rasta art earthquake, lightning, and thunder!"

"Aba!" someone called out.

"Liquidate--" Bongo U said.

"Thunder!"

"-- the plan of the dragon and crash the ways of Babylon. And set up a foundation of purity, that each and every eye shall behold Selassie I as the Almighty. It takes divine consciousness to stand before my father. My father are not mere curiosity, he is reality. His Imperial Majesty, Emperor Haile Selassie stand upon the threshold of judgement. One foot upon the sea, one upon the land, for judgment did come!

"Selassie I will never forsake I and I. He shall always be with I and I with him. Because the foundation of holiness have been made. It never been moved from creation. Is man move from those qualities. It abideth forever. For as long as there is Time and there is Nature and there is Space, holiness still reigneth.

"Is man want to remove those ancient landmarks of purity, but they have failed. Because they are seeking of that place now. And cannot reach there. Because have gone to the moon. And one time Englishmen say heaven was behind the moon one time, now he say nothing again, just some rockstone up there, which I know they didn't go upon my mother, and the moon is my mother. They are a notorious liar! They are only trying to deceive Israel by their power! Tower of Babel! But Rasta in here!   To tell them is a lie. Because is the second tower of Babel they are building again. Moonwalkers. To which there is no hiding place up there. Because my Father come to blast them down! My Father would never build a house and live above it. On top of it. He dwell within this earth as a solid foundation. The divine spirit of I and I Father dwelleth and reigneth in the hearts of those who try and do his will-- his work.

"And there is no planets up there effect man, because the twelve constellation zodiac are the twelve sons of Jacob, but the western hemisphere call them planets, so they want to lost Israel path. The twelve months also are the twelve son that have formed creation out of the abscess of a woman's womb.

"There are certain God-like qualities of love, purity, holiness, and unity in each and every man. Don't matter how he say he is an atheist or an evolutionist. There are certain tendencies, certain qualities in him that pronounce good, that germinate at all times the things that is natural to his own desire. I and I, the Rasta, know that the pagan out there on a whole couldn't take the Almighty Selassie I as God. Because their eyes have been clouded with their visions of lust and vanities and greed, which cause their desires to fulfill in pain and sorrow. They have no solution to those dangerous monster to which they cause to infiltrate their hearts. Those dangerous monster are greed, lust, desire-- fulfillment of one's own appetite.

"The man who create this earth did create it not for himself alone, but for Nature and Space. He create it so that his children and his woman shall have abundant lands to play upon, and to have sufficient to fill his appetite and satisfy his desire. But the ways of Babylon have changed the course of paradise!"

"Babylon is the western world?" Jack asked.

"Yes. The ways of *Jeesus*, which is money and power. Because *Jeesus* have take everything and fill his own mouth and fill his *lactorious* gut! And cause him to be like a big tree that produceth no fruit. And the small fruit them that are genuine, that can fill the nations' appetite, his wide wings, which is his branches covered, that stop it from grow. That is *Jeesus*.

"The only way one can exist in this society, or within this constitution to which Shearer the prime minister have been draw, have been borrowed from the colonial governments, you have to find yourself within their society and bow to the threshold of churches, and prostitute oneself for the likeness of money that one man may fall in the high seat of crown and title, of fame and power-- at the same time trampling His good name under the brutal feet of might, and take his own skin as the cheapest formality of human commerce.

"Because from the foundation, there was three sins that fight against Selassie I in the garden of Eden, which is Mount Zion. It was comb, scissor, and razor. They are one named commerce, politics, and religion. England, Russia, and America. One named democracy, colonialism, and communism. All three of them have built a revolutionary force upon creation, upon earth, which is the western hemisphere. And have built a tower of false literature to give Israel so that they have no culture of their own to call upon.

Must be the black man who teach them own culture. Then if the white man want to participate, him free, because the black man is full of love, charity, and humility, So the black man call all unto him and separate the good from the bad, just as our Father shall sit on his white tribunal of judgment, to judge the quick and the dead. The quick shall be I and I, and the dead, the living dead out there. The earth will come to a perpetual standstill."

This worried me. "Yeah, within ten years?" I asked.

"Within every two thousand year dispensation, for the dawning of the new world is about to come! And in this third and last dispensation, the dawning of the new world will be life. Live everliving, which no seed shall die. All will be made perfect, but who shall endure to enter through the portal of the new Jerusalem! I and I, the sheep-like people who have been sent by Selassie I down through creation gathered back Israel to their culture. Whosoever will, shall come."

"Prophecy must fulfill," said Kingman.

"Aba!" said Sherer.

I looked at Jack and he at me. Bongo U walked outside his cardboard house and stood before the Caribbean Sea, which had been calmly coming in and going out just within the range of my hearing. As I said, I only understood half of what was said because of the patois-inflected language and the emphatic way of speaking. Jack was held spellbound too, even understanding less than I, who had been to the island several times before.

A bongo man named Maxy had been cooking in a large pot over an open fire, and Rastamen began bringing out ancient *gourdi* bowls made from the shell of a fruit sometimes as large as a basketball. The bowls were filled with steaming rice, red peas cooked in grated fresh coconut milk, *callilou* greens cooked with tomato, onion, coconut oil, scallion, and red pepper. There was no salt in the food. Jack and I were given a bowl.

The pepper was hot and the food was filling, tasting like no vegetables I had ever eaten. Darkness began to fill in the space before the sea. Jack waited while I enjoyed another cigar.

"Love," Jack said.

"Love I," said Kingman.

"Love Rasta," said Bongo U.

Jack and I left, walking along the sea. The sounds eased a mind overworked, overtired, and what you might call spaced by Bongo U's "cosmically speaking." We did not say anything to each other, because there didn't seem like much else that could be said. Along the edge of the sea in little clearings, or under trees in the brush alongside the beach, flames and seeds popped and cracked as Rastamen drew their herb, showering sparks of fire into the darkness.

We met a man named Lloyd who had short hair and smooth face. Lloyd said he was an acrobat for the tourist clubs uptown. He had come down the beach to mellow out some. He said he had seven wives, and we knew that many Jamaicans do not marry, but move in with a woman and give her children as long as it is comfortable. Lloyd said he had fourteen children, which at one time gave him a certain amount of worry, until he developed his mind to a point where matter could no longer stand as an obstacle before him. Mind over matter. Most of Lloyd's problems were therefore solved without his having to take an active physical part in them. There was now, he said, sufficient moneys and food to care for all his family. Yea, right, I thought.

Somehow we made it back to Percy's at Mount Salem. We were exhausted physically and mentally, about to fall into a deep sleep in the loft we had built above Percy's oven in the bakery. Peace at last, at least for a short time.

And Jack had seen what Jamaica can do to the consciousness of man, stretched and pushed to the ultimate in fantasy, reality, prophecy, visions, and what the Rasta call "reasoning", until our western minds could no longer function their rational acceptance of the order of the universe.

We lay on the shelf above the brick oven, listening to all the dogs holler at each other. We had said good night to Percy, and climbed up onto the rounded dome top of the oven and then into the loft. The loft had been nailed into a corner and supported by a bamboo pole as thick as a leg, which we had carried up from the river where bamboo grows fifty foot tall, looking fern- or featherlike from a distance, green, sometimes fifty or a hundred stalks climbing at the sky.

Water at the river flows over a dam and down into a clear pool. When we were cutting the bamboo for our loft, two Jamaican men stood naked, knee-deep at the edges of the stream, washing out their underwear and spreading it out on the bushes. The women were doing their laundry a little further down the river, pounding the soapy clothes on a rock to make the dirt come out, they said.

Percy's man George had come with us and climbed twelve feet or so up the bamboo. He whacked it off with his machete. We trimmed it up, then carried it up the hill and along the commons. White birds picked the ticks off brown and black cows, lifted into the air and floated down along the hill before drifting into treetops along the way to wait until we had passed.

Lying in the loft, Jack said, "I wish I could have understood more of what Bongo U was saying. I have a feeling he was making logical sense most of the time, but I can't be sure."

"Don't feel bad," I said. "I've been here before, and heard the language a lot more than you have, and still there was a lot of it I couldn't hear. And at times I just stopped listening. I'm not used to hearing that much stuff at one time. We've got the cassette, and I'll translate it for us when we get back to America."

"Those Rastas sure have a lot to say," Jack said.

"You could say that. I don't think I could listen to another thought."

I heard the jukebox. There is a little bar next to Percy's, called the "Happy Landing." The guy there sells eighteen cent beers and strong white rum-- overproof, nicknamed "Devil soup." He stays open as long as there is someone to drink and talk with him. Some nights it is day before he closes, music plays all night. Rasta songs, too. Just when I thought I had heard all I could hear, across the air it came:

"Oh let the power fall on I and I,
let the power fall on I.
Let the power from Zion fall on I,
let the power fall on I.

Oh give I justice, peace and love for I,
give I justice, peace and love,

How long will the wicked reign for I,
Give I justice, peace and love.

So let the power fall on I for I,
let the power fall on I
    (oh Zion)   (praise the Lord!)
Oh let the power from Zion fall on I,
let the power fall on I.

Oh let the wicked burn in flames for I,
let the wicked burn in flames.
Oh let the wicked burn to ash for I,
let the wicked burn in flames.

And let the power fall on I for I,
let the power fall on I.
Let the power from Zion fall on I,
let the power fall on I."

There was silence for a minute, or, should I say, dogs barking. The next song was something like "Lion of Judah going to break every chain/ Lion of Judah again and again."

It must have been nearly midnight when we fell asleep, still hearing but no longer able to listen. No telling how long the music or the talk went on. It is probably still going on, while you read this. Probably just a new version.

CRASHED CAR

A few years later Bongo U asks me to rent him a car car so he and his bredren could go to a large Rasta gathering at Bull Bay outside of Kingston He said the rental people do not like to rent to Rasta, and you will shortly find out why. I was picked up in the pre dawn darkness, gulped down some coffee and mistakenly put cream in it . Then I ate an orange and the acid curdled with the cream when the driver speed shifted and took all the corners fast and sharp rocking me from one side of the car to the other I had to stop the car and puke among the lush tropical foliage with the pale blue Caribbean sea in the distance. Bongo U was very annoyed and strolled calmly about gathering some leafy plants for herbal remedies. looking quite regal while he was doing it What did he want me to do? Puke in the car? Two hours passed among the drumming and chanting. Bongo U and I walked past all the parked, and one was trashed. "That guy shure had a bad wreck" Roof dented, windshield gone, passenger side steer pealed back showing guts of the door mechanisms and no windowglass at all.

"Is same cyar yunno", says Bongo U "IS SAME CAR" I shouted because I did not even recognize the new Toyota I rented earlier. I read the fine print that says insurance is invalid if someone else is driving the car. "Just tell them you were driving"

"WELL I'M DRIVING NOW", I said forcefully, and slid in behind the steering wheel. I put on my shades, and the Rasta posse crowded in. Just outside Kingston, a huge overloaded diesel gravel truck was in front of me, toiling up the hill - loose gravel and oily smoke allowed inside the car by lack of windshield. I felt gravel popping against my shade, so I floorboarded it, raced around the truck leaning heavily on the horn because I couldn't see if it was safe to pass. " Boy, me nevva know white man could drive", said a backseat Rasta. Back in Mobay I unloaded the Rastas, and headed to the airport to return the Toyota.

"I got into a wreck," I said. "No you didn't she said. A rival rental car employee told me this car sideswiped a parked bus, overturned with Rastas climbing out the windshield shaking broken glass from their locks. The bus passengers helped flip the car back on its wheels, and the Rastas raced back to Bull Bay to give me a wrecked car to return.

ISEMBLE REASONING

"You raped my sister, you motherfucker! I'm going to slit your throat!" he shouted to me, one of the first dreadlocked white men.

"I don't even know your sister," I said.

"You *pussyclot*! I'm going to kill you," screamed the dreadlocked black man.

Ten or twelve men sat around on locks listening. Kingstonian Rastas. One man moved three logs closer to the heart of the fire. Yams were slowly roasting. An old Rasta with full and gray lock lay in a hammock suspended in the shade of two trees.

"What do you have there?" The old man was looking at the tape recorder.

"Last night's chanting and *aketta*," I said.

"Let I hear it," he said.

I punched the "on" button and handed the tape recorder to him. He set it on his stomach and after awhile he smiled and lay back listening.

"Why do you have it? To make money in America?"

"I am not a *Jeesus bwoy*. These chants give inspiration."

He seemed satisfied with the answer.

"You dirty cocksucker anthropologist! I'll slit your fucking throat, you honky bastard!" My assailant did not smile when he spoke. The dozen or so men sitting around did not taking sides. They just listened to see what would happen.

"*Pussyclot* motherfucker!"

"You may wear long locks and precepts, but you can't fool anyone," I said. "The Rasta come from love and unity, and all the *bredren* have to do is look upon your face full of hate to see you are no Rasta. Imitation Rastaman!" I shouted.

Rage now took over where his anger left off, but the man didn't move from the rock. The old man smiled and the men sitting around murmured because the Rasta love a good argument, or "reasoning." The enraged man and I both knew the men were taking no sides.

"You pussysucker!" he said. But his voice did not have the same degree of intensity and he began to calm down. Still the old man lay back with the machine on his belly, listening.

"Your mother's a stinking whore!" he went on.

Near me a man was folding a shirt slowly and carefully into a small suitcase. He looked over at me and said gently, "If you do not have tolerance, you can never find perseverance."

"Love Rasta," I said quietly.

"Love Selassie I," he said.

The old man looked pleased.

Chanting: "With clean hands and a pure heart, I must *see Jah. Aketta*!"

Near the drummers, on a little hill under a small shade tree, another black man sat. Long gray locks fell all over his shoulders, tumbling past his elbows. There were three younger rastamen sitting beside him. When I passed he shouted, "Hey, *hippi*! *Way* you go?" His face was bright as a happy child.

I turned and faced him. "Rude *bwoy!*" I shouted. He smiled as I approached. "Are you one of those rude *bwoys* I've been hearing so much about?"

"So then, you are no screwface, I see," he said. "Where do you stay? To what country do you belong?"

"I was born in America, but a man's country is where his heart is and where many people greet him with love."

"Do you stay in a hotel?"

"No. I have been staying two months in a small house in Catadupa, in the hills. We prepare our own food--*callilou* and yams and green banana porridge."

"Then you are a Jamaican!"

"So *you* say."

"True," he said. "Now the man expects that at a certain time there will be the return of a Man that trod the earth about two thousand years ago. See? Called *Jeasus Christus,* or *Jeasus* Christ. And he was *Negus.* Black--from the tribe of Judah. Right? And now the man expect that Man going to trod back this earth at some time?"

"Sure," said I.

"At about what time does this man expect that Man to drod back the earth?" he asked.

"I don't know."

"All right. The man doesn't know anything about the significance of this two thousand years that has expired? The man never heard any teaching about the significance of that two thousand years?"

"No."

"Seen. Now, the first time when this great king trod on this earth-- He trod lots of time before, you know, but I and I talking about when He trod now and they crucify him as the *Negus.* Because over His cross them add I N R I--Iasus Nazaretum, Rex Israel--is that Man I talking about now. When He trod the first time, raise up on the earth at that time was the greatest power, military power on earth. Before them had Greece, Persia, Babylon, but none of them could come to the might of the Roman Empire. Is the leg of iron that Daniel *Prophasl* about."

"The Roman Empire is that leg of iron?"

"Seen. The man read the prophecy of Daniel? The man is conversant with that prophecy? Of Daniel?"

"Not specifically."

"When he had the dream. And he saw a statue with a head of gold, chest and arms of silver, middle of bronze, legs of iron, toes mixed with clay and iron. I can read it for the man later in the Bible. Seen? Nebuchadezzar had that dream, you know, and he couldn't *I-terpret* it. He call all the famous *majicians* and *chaldereans,* and they couldn't *I-terpret* it. But in the land at that time in captivity was Daiel, of I and I. Sight? Out of the same tribe as I and I in that time. Now they had to call him to *I-terpret* the dream, and he *I-terpret* it that Nebuchadnezzar's kingdom, Babylon, was represented by the head of gold after that would rise up a kingdom of less value, represented by silver, which is Persia, showing two arms, is a double kingdom that. Seen. After that now, it will be Greece, which you know it was Alexander conquered Mede and Persia. After that will be the legs of iron that would trample everything because it is more powerful than all the metals before yet it is baser. That was Rome.

"I see."

"Because Rome conquer Greece."

"Most of the known world."

"True. Then out of Rome now ten tribes descend out of the hills and caves of Europe. Seen? Descend upon the kingdom of Rome and tear it to pieces. So you find now instead of two legs of iron, you have ten toes now representing the ten tribes that trod out of the hills of Europe. Seen. those were the Asghots and the Eruli, and all them tribes there. So that was the ten. Represented those days by the ten main countries of Europe. Seen? That they gathering in a common market thing in these days. Is the same people. Sight?"

"Mmmhmm."

"But in revelation now, then after that now, take over and show that another beast rise, and by the *I-terpretation* of those beasts it will show you that the beast that rise after that, him rise out of the ten, so that was the Pope, who carry--because the Vatican between the time of Rome and up to and up to about eighteen hundred--because it was the Vatican through the Papal government did rule the whole of Europe and all the colonized peoples also. But that was out of the ten still. Then after that it show that another beast rose. And that other beast now come up out of the land. Not out of the sea like the other beast rose."

We could hear the *aketta* drumming and the chants of hundreds of Rastamen.

"End of different types of government coming down to this time. Right? So I and I know by the time it get back to the feet, you know what time of government has come, because the foot is the end of the structure, which is supposed to be after God, or *jah*. Seen?"

"Sure."

"So this is why you hear the said Age of Aquarius is rising. Because after the foot comes what? Must be the head."

"Begins again."

"Truly. So then I and I now know that at that time a king came, you know, and trod the earth, a powerful king. *I Negus Christus*. Because the most powerful, dread, corrupted empire was founded at that time. If Him never trod at that time they would completely scorch the earth. But the prophecies weren't fulfilled, so it couldn't happen at that time. The next dread time is when the next dread beast seated upon--that is the United States of America. Why the United States of America is so dread is because they pretend to be like lamb, as I and I when they uphold the slavery and economic bondage of earlier beasts who sucked the blood of the sufferers also."

THE INDIANS ARE COMING!

The Apache and Dine' came up from New Mexico, Blackfeet down from Alberta and Montana, the Yuma east from California. From the Black Hills of South Dakota came the Lakota Sioux, then the Mohawks from the east. From over 80 tribes they came to worship in the Southern Illinois Ozarks as part of The Longest Walk. They traveled for thousands of miles, from every direction, to pray for the understanding and education of the white man, to pray for their fallen ancestors along the infamous "Trail of Tears," and to pray for Leonard Peltier, jailed at Marion Federal Pen.

I came from Boskydell, just fifteen minutes away. I had been minding my own business, tucked away on a small farm, worrying about the spring grass growing tall beside the broken riding mower. I was thinking about the beetles that were already chomping on my young lettuce. All of a sudden, in the mailbox was a flyer from a friend relaying the cry: <u>The Indians are coming!</u> The Longest Walk was nearly in my backyard.

Big deal, my garden had its own weeds. I went on about the business of finding a lamb to carry for the Caribbean Student Association, of which I am a charter member. I finally found a lamb, and at the feast a round and smiley Jamaican woman told me a minister named Fred Krauss, from St. Peter's United Church of Christ, wanted to talk to me about getting another lamb for some function or other, she didn't know what. I'd forgotten all about the Indians by then, as one is apt to do. This minister, however, asked me if I could find another spring lamb to give to the Indians as part of an offering from his flock. The minister said he did not know if it was to be used for sacrifice or for food, so he kind of left it up to me.

Red Hill, the farmer, had another fat lamb. He also said he'd sell the ewe, too, but she didn't look too appetizing, just coming off from milking that same lamb I finally decided to buy. I tied the lamb's feet and put him in the bed of the '52 Dodge pickup, along with a hundred-pound sack of potatoes and fifty pounds of onions. I hooked up a small camper behind the truck, hoping there wouldn't be any problem getting a live lamb into Ferne Clyffe State Park, the Indian's campground. Thought there'd be some kind of law against it.

The old Dodge pulled into the park around noon on Monday, May 15, 1978, and drove to the group camping area. Sure enough, there were two Indians. They stood beside a bright red '57 Apache truck from the state of New Mexico. After Yellow Man saw the sheep, potatoes, and onions in the back of the truck, he found a place to park the camper, behind a thorny locust tree, near his orange tent.

Yellow Man had made the front page of the St. Louis paper, in color, gathering up his sleeping gear in the rain beneath the stainless steel arch. It's a good thing that the camper was parked before the Indians set up their security, because the next day security was so tight that very few men not known to the Indians were allowed into the campsite. That often included this white man, when important meetings were held.

"He's not very big," said Moose, speaking about the lamb.

"We can still eat him," offered a second Indian.

"We can take him in the bushes right now," said Yellow Man, touching the sheath of his knife.

"We better wait 'til Tishka gets here. He'll know what to do," said Moose. He unloaded the lamb, hitching him to a sapling by a rope tied to one foreleg.

Yellow Man helped park my camper. We had just freed it from the truck when a dusty old beater of a station wagon full of Indians drove by. They had a bundle of willow poles tied to the roof. Green leaves waved like flags behind the car-- even though most of the poles were stripped clean, a few branches remained at the top. There was a scrap of red cloth tied to the antenna, flapping with the motion of the car. Many of the support vehicles for The Walk had the same red symbol.

"They're going to build the sweats," said Yellow Man.

"Sweats?"

"The sweat lodges. You want to see how we make them?"

We hopped in the old Dodge. Yellow Man directed me to an overgrown, unused part of the park, where eight warriors stood near two sweat lodges. One frame was already covered with patched canvas. In the old days, I found out, they had used half-worn-out buffalo hides. A man drove holes in the ground for the second sweat with an iron crowbar. He made four holes corresponding to the four corners of the universe, and he bent the supple willowpoles toward the center, wrapping the small ends around each other, forming an arch four foot high, tied with honeysuckle vines. Then two more toward the east and west. A total of sixteen poles were slipped into the wet ground, wrapped and tied in a similar manner, until a shell was made to support the canvas. Bucky Fuller would have been delighted to see the creation of the ancient prototype of his famous dome. That form and those triangles were among the Redman since before history.

Someone told me to clear the path of brambles and briars, a path that would later be walked smooth by hundreds of feet day and night. The Indians performed ceremonies of purification, traditional songs, and prayer. Between the canvas-covered domes a huge fire was to be built, with loads of rocks piled on top.

A security person asked what I was doing there. He told me I should have asked permission to set up camp. When he learned there was a chainsaw in the camper, he and I spent the rest of the afternoon cutting wood for the sweat lodge fires.

Sandstone bluffs rise on the east edge of Ferne Clyffe Park. The water to make coffee was near the main cooking area. In the late afternoon the main tribes had yet to arrive. I showed a woman an arrowhead dug up on my farm, a holy stone relic. She told me she always wanted one to wear around her neck. I gave it to her. A huge white van drove up. It looked like an old fashioned milk truck, but a dozen bald headed men in flowing orange robes began drumming and chanting in the distance, where the truck had gone. I thought it was the Hare Krishna people.

"The Buddhists are here! The Buddhists are here!" said the head cook, Regina Brave Dixon, who now owned a Southern Illinois arrowhead. "Go and welcome them," she told the kids, as she stirred the large flat pan of potatoes frying oven an open fire. Long-haired Indian children ran up to the Buddhists, laughing, happy to see them. The bald headed monks greeted the Indians with a polite bow, clasped hands, palms together, fingers to the sky. I learned later that they were Bodhisattvas seeking enlightenment. Two young Buddhists, Nezume and Shegeki, had been with The Longest Walk since Alcatraz, and others stopped by only overnight to add their prayers to those of the Indians. The main body of monks had flown into San Francisco from Japan, and they were on their way to New York to welcome their leader, the 93-year-old Most Venerable Fujii Guruji, who was to present Dr. Kurt Waldheim, Secretary General of the United Nations, with 20 million signatures of the world's people, calling for the elimination of nuclear weapons on May 30, 1975, two weeks from today. Fujii Guruji promised to meet with the Indians shortly afterward. I found out he had been invited by Dennis Banks to join The Longest Walk.

Most Venerable Nichidatsun Fujii:

We have just spoken with Shigeki who has returned from The Longest Walk, which is halfway across the country. The Longest Walk is constituted of 600 Native Americans and non-Indians alike who have pledged to walk to Washington, DC, to protest the eleven pieces of anti-Indian legislation which have been introduced in the U.S. Congress to abrogate all Indian treaties, to destroy all fishing and water rights, all introduced for one purpose: To terminate Native Americans. Most importantly of all, The Longest Walk is a Spiritual Walk.

Shigeki has informed us that you will be arriving in the United States on May 23rd. It would be a great honor for us if you could please join The Longest Walk at this time, or whenever your schedule would permit. Many of our people have heard about you and it would be a great honor if you could stop by and be with us a few minutes.

Thank you for all your prayers and support already.

Respectfully,
Dennis J. Banks

Unlike Fujii Guruji, I came to The Longest Walk uninvited. Shigeki said that he must be a part of The Longest Walk because he felt it was a historically important event-- a walk in prayer for peace across the face of one of the world's chief supplier of arms.

I reasoned with the monks. One of them presented me with a gift-- a trail-worn rainwater-curled picture book about a Sri Lanka peace pagoda. I took the book to the camper, made coffee, filled the thermos, and took it back to the sweat lodge area. I helped Moose unload stones from the bed of his brother's Apache pickup. The Indians lay three-foot-long logs on the earth facing north and south. Then they piled on another tier east and west, with small pieces of wood and kindling between the logs. They repeated this until the woodpile neared three feet tall. Dozens of stones were placed on top of the pile, and then more wood was stacked around in the four directions, looking like a miniature tipi. You could barely see any of the stones.

The ground was on a slight hill, so the Indians leveled the earth and used the clods to seal where the canvas covering the sweat lodges touched the ground.

The sun began to go down. I was hungry from all the woodcutting, stone carrying, and lamb buying. I walked the mile along the winding and deserted park access road back to the campsite. Honeysuckle and wild raspberry blossoms scented the air. A heavy mist was falling from a gray and heavy sky. Whippoorwills were starting to call when I heard the drums. It sounded like hundreds of them echoing from the surrounding hills, but the drum rhythms were completely new to me. At that time I didn't know that they didn't look like drums at all, and had been made thousands of miles away, by yellow, rather than red, men.

The sound of chanting grew louder at the top of the hill overlooking the campgrounds. Bright orange as poppies in the green spring grass near the edge of the gravel sat over a dozen monks. An altar with a golden statue of the Buddha face the setting sun past the drizzling rain. The chill of early evening was all around us. A banner made in Japan, a sun of gold in the center of a purple field, moved in the breeze over the altar.

A couple of Indians stood around staring like Anglo tourists at a Sun Dance. Moose showed up. A monk on the edge of the bright orange covey twinkled at Moose, and tried to hand him a *fan tieko* and a smooth stick of wood to strike it with, but Moose seemed a little self-conscious and declined at first. Moose had more sense than I. I accepted the heavenly drum with the mantra painted around its circular face in bold, hand-painted Japanese characters: "Namu Myoho Renge Kyo." Little Moose and I didn't know it then, but this is what the Buddhists were chanting. We'd never heard of, nor seen a *fan tieko* before. It looks like a twelve-inch round Ping-Pong paddle, with what appeared to be animal hide stretched tight to a wooden frame, with the handle below it. We held them toward the setting sun, now hidden behind the heavy rain clouds.

I took off my shoes and put them between me and the wet grass. I used the stick of wood to sound the drum, trying to stay with the constant rhythm and chanting of the Buddhist monks. At first I missed some beats. The monk who'd given it to me looked encouraging, and he showed me again-- four long beats and then three quick ones, over and over. If I stopped he would smile kindly at me, so I concentrated. And concentrated. Until I realized I was stuck. I couldn't just get up and walk away from the altar before they finished, and darkness was closing in fast. I shook my head fiercely to scare off mosquitoes. Rain fell harder. I did the best I could.

When my buddy Moose saw me trying, he took up the *fan tieko* waiting in the grass for him. He sat behind the group on a picnic bench and missed lots of beats. His wrong beats sounded loud and out of place. Then he began to do better. The monks chanted and drummed the same mantra over and over, for nearly an hour. One would stop for a moment to shoo a mosquito off his bald head, and got right on drumming.

Finally my mind freed itself of all the miscellaneous thoughts that were causing me to skip beats, or to add one out of place. It was dark and raining harder when horns blasted and car lights blinked. The *fan tiekos* sounded louder and louder. The Indians whooped and shouted as scores of support vehicles carrying the main tribes of The Longest Walk pulled in a long caravan up the winding roads of Ferne Clyffe Park.

How rude to disturb the praying monks, I thought. The Indians in the cars waved and shouted greetings to the Buddhists, who then chanted still louder. The entire camping area filled with the clamor of hundreds of people setting up tents and getting boiled coffee from huge pots over the open-pit fires. Laughter and greetings could be heard from those who had just joined up with the walk. Some would return home after the ceremonies, others would continue all the way to the nation's capital.

A huge tipi was set up in the glare of car headlights. Eighteen-foot-tall poles were leaned against one another, and a white canvas covering was stretched tight around the poles. Hundreds of smaller pup tents sprang up everywhere, right up to the door of my camper. The young lamb was still tied to a sassafras sapling nearby, hiding in the bushes from all the excitement. I stumbled over tent lines in the dark to have a closer look at the great tipi covered with paintings. The top was painted red, and its opening faced the east. The Buddhists vanished, into their tents and white van, I guessed.

*****

"There I was, with a tank of gas and fifteen dollars in my pocket, separated from my caravan, a thousand miles from California," one Indian said to another.

"How'd you finally make it?"

"Called lots of churches and explained about the spiritual walk to help our people. And finally a Christian helped me to get here.

*****

"I filled the bowl of my sacred pipe in California and vowed that I would not smoke or eat until I reached The Longest Walk."

*****

"Did you hear what Amtrak promised?"

"I heard they phoned."

"A free ride home from The Walk. Telephone and hearsay. I'll believe it when I see it. They are supposed to send a letter."

"I'll believe it when the ticket home is in my hand."

"They gonna pack the busses on flatcars?"

"Supposed to."

"Don't hold your breath. You'll be a dead Indian."

*****

Tuesday, May 16, 1978. Overcast sky at dawn. The sun had not yet come up over the sandstone bluffs. A deep, coarse voice shouted, "Cock A-Doodle-Doo! Cock A-Doodle-Doo!" It was a two hundred pound rooster with a round belly. He stomped up and down the sleeping campground hollering at the top of his big voice. "I said Cock A-Doodle-DOO! Get up! Everybody up! COCK A-DOODLE-DOO! NO LAZY INDIANS ON THIS WALK!" Thump, thump, he kicked at the taut tent lines as he made his way through the awakening camp. Thump. Thump. "Cock A-Doodle-Doo!"

I woke up laughing at the fat rooster. I might not have laughed so hard had I known that he was a pipe carrier, one who had suffered the Sun Dance for his people.

Indian heads popped out of tent flaps, blinking at the white mist covering the little valleys of the gently rolling Southern Illinois countryside. Ernie Peters, leader of the walk, and the other spiritual leaders were off in a quiet place, I found out later, praying with the Pipe at dawn. As their fathers had done for over a thousand years. Traditional songs could already be heard in the sweat lodges. The fire for heating rocks would burn for three days and three nights. The same fire.

Black-haired women put enamel coffee pots over cook fires started by borrowing hot coals from the main fire near the large tipi. It had been burning all night long. Most everyone was fully awake by now. Children played in the wet grass. A few came over to look at the lamb, still tied by a foreleg, now used to his tether.

A small voice said, "Get out! Get out!" to a rat-sized dog trying to sniff the lamb's behind. The dog scared the lamb back into the bushes.

"Stop it, Worms! I said stop! Get out of there!"

"That's his name?" I asked, "Worms?"

"Yeah."

"You give him that name?"

"You mean Worms? No. My momma named her. I have a different name."

"What's that?"

"Penny."

"Has she never seen a sheep before?"

"Nope."

Three kids pet the lamb while a fourth held Worms in his hands. The children were on The Longest Walk as part of their Survival School, a school of traditional Indian culture and values. The walk was part of their education, as well as part of a historically important event for Native Americans.

I remembered my three dreams and I wanted to find Ernie Peters and talk to him about the meaning. One of the kids said he'd seen him over by the Sioux camp toward the east. The sun had warmed the chill of early dawn. Large birds floated in the rising air above us. Kermit, a security man, offered me some boiled coffee from an antique and battered enamel pot. It was strong and eye-opening. Three other men stood around the fire. Kermit sat on a green picnic bench. The sounds of Buddhist drums covered the hills. Coffee steamed in Kermit's cup.

One of the Indians searched the sky. Birds with black and white wings circled high above the rock bluffs toward the east. "There's our leader," said one Indian.

"The eagle," said another, proudly.

"That's no eagle," said Kermit.

"Sure it is. It must be."

I knew for sure what it was, but I kept silent. Kermit said, "I tell you, that's no eagle. Eagles don't fly like that."

The birds flapped heavily in the morning air. We all looked up, including three kids. I said nothing. Kermit said, "An eagle don't flip-flop his wings like that."

"He's trying to gain the heights."

"Maybe it's some kind of Missouri buzzard," Kermit said. He turned to me. "What do you think it is? You live around here. You're supposed to know."

"Buzzards, I think," I said quietly. The Indians were silent for a long time. Then one man looked me dead in the eye. "I remember one time at a Sun Dance, this big Indian said he saw an eagle in the sky. No one would tell him we knew it was a buzzard."

Suddenly afraid, I thought before I spoke. "If a man is truly strong, he is never afraid of the truth." As soon as possible I retreated to the main cooking area where Regina Brave Dixon was again stirring potatoes. She was also taking care of a little girl, about three years old. "The young men are too soft these days," she chided those who huddled around waiting for breakfast. "In the old days we raised boys to be men, and now we raise babies to be boys!" Then she added, "We need more firewood over here!" goading the men into action with her tongue. Within twenty minutes a large stack of firewood was split and stacked neatly near the cooking area. There were fried potatoes and eggs for all those who felt like eating. Many of the Indians fasted for Leonard Peltier, as I did, having been asked to do so by the pipe carriers and medicine men in the circle ceremony at dawn.

*****

It was the day of the rally for Leonard Peltier. Early in the morning, six Indians brought their sacred bundles wrapped in soft deerskin to the southeast corner of the campgrounds. The five men and a woman were pipe carriers, people who hold a position of honor and esteem among traditional Indians. A large ring of people began to form loosely, slowly growing larger with each new member. The ring circled the leaders, who unpacked their natural religious symbols with the reverence of a priest when he handles the chalice, a rabbi the Torah, the Muslim his Quran, the Buddhist monk his prayer drum.

"You Christians use the cross," Ernie Peters said later that day to the Associated Press reporter, outside the prison gates at Marion. "We, the Indian people, use only things from our Mother Earth. You white people call us savages. I am proud to be a savage!" The reporter gulped.

The growing circle contained four races of people-- a black man with African ancestors, Japanese monks, Indians from all over North America, and a handful of Anglos, originally from Europe. Some traditional Indians believe their prayers will be strong if every color of humanity is properly represented. Others believe the prayer is weakened by the presence of a white man.

During The Longest Walk, the pipe carriers always moved in front of the people. Then came the banners, then the drummers and those chanting, then the people in a group, flanked by security people for protection. As far as anyone knew on Tuesday morning, no one would be allowed inside the prison to see the man who helped bring together nearly five hundred Indians, as well as the Buddhist monks, to fill the hills of Southern Illinois with the sounds of drums, *fan tiekos*, chants, and prayers to a God of many names.

Jeff Weiss and Jim Roberts, young and dedicated white lawyers based in Carbondale, backed up by imported Boston legal clout Lew Gurlwitz, worked day and night to secure the freedom of Leonard Peltier to meet with his spiritual leaders. The Indians, the Buddhists, and I drove toward the Marion Federal Penitentiary in old school busses, pickups, vans, and cars. We were met with a police barricade a mile from the prison, near the Grange Hall Free Will Baptist Church. There were lots of clean-cut white men with two-way radios. Six state police cars were parked in a row. Charlie Roberts, the Associated Press correspondent from Centralia, was on the scene. Charlie couldn't seem to count any higher than two hundred and fifty. Since all the Indians were lined up in a close formation, I could count off twenty five in a ten-foot piece of one lane of the road, and then count in groups of twenty-five. But no, the press coverage said 250. Ernie Peters said later that when you see Indians, it's kinda like an iceberg. You only see the visible ones. There were many who remained in camp that day.

Cars and busses packed the church parking lot. Hundreds of Indians lined up east of the roadblock behind their pipe carriers, and their colorful red, yellow, black, and blue banners. Some women wore heavy velvet skirts that reached the ground. Some men wore spotted eagle feathers in their long hair or attached to the staffs they carried, so that they spun in the air as if alive.

The drums rang loud when struck with buffalo hide-covered sticks, the hair side out. Chanting and singing of ancient songs began. A white man spoke into his radio, "Blue Two to Blue One. Red car coming through." State policemen removed the barricade.

The lone red Chevy Vega with a big white buffalo skull on the roof track slowly carried Ernie Peters and Greg Zephier down the empty stretch of blacktop toward the top security United States Federal Penitentiary at Marion, Illinois. Over four hundred Indians remained behind with their pipe carriers and drummers. Almost everyone was singing. Leonard Peltier's three year old daughter moved freely among the people. First she walked near the great drum, then out in front, then off to the side near the tall grass. She was gently brought into the group by an Indian security man who stood between the white onlookers and the tribes.

Around noon Charlie Roberts walked past the barricade and headed down the empty stretch toward the prison. The lone red car had already disappeared behind the gently rolling hills. A hundred yards behind Mr. Roberts walked the AP cameraman, awkwardly carrying all his gear. Then came a short man in a Levi's jacket loaded down with camera equipment. He limped heavily as he walked in stiff boots. We walked together along the empty road for a short while.

"Hi," I said. He said nothing. "You with the Indians?" Again, nothing. "Are you free-lance?" He walked steadily forward. His face told me nothing. "I'm trying to write a story," I said. Still nothing. "You think they'll let anyone in to see Peltier?"

Meadowlarks warbled in distant fields. White Fox limped silently in the direction of the second barricade set up especially for the Indians, so far away from the prison that all you could see was the water tower rising above it. Later White Fox would prevent me from re-entering the camp.

By the time we reached the iron gate, the buffalo skull, bleached white by the hot western sun, was resting in the knee-high deep green grass of late spring. The black horns curved away from the prison toward the south.

Ernie Peters, Greg Zephier, Leonard Crow Dog, and two other pipe carriers took their sacred objects from soft buckskin bundles and arranged them carefully around the altar. They took sage from a plastic bag outside the altar area and arranged it in an ancient manner, placing it under the pipes and in the eye sockets of the buffalo skull.

It looked like there were at least four kinds of cops on the west side of the iron gate. Half a dozen federal marshals wore pale blue jumpsuits over bulletproof vests. There was one state policeman in a brown uniform, possible a couple of FBI men in neat suits and ties, two men in low-profile Levi's, and a couple of local good old boys, maybe guards. White Fox snapped their pictures. The country boy cops talked about their gardens. One neatly spit tobacco juice. I talked briefly to them, convincing some of the Walk security that I was a planted spy of the FBI.

From over the hills toward the east we could hear the drums. They seemed to be getting louder by the minute. All the pipe carriers appeared out in front of all 80 tribes, slowly walking and singing over the rounded hills. The drums grew louder. Southern Illinois country folk on their front porches watched and listened. Some sipped coffee. Some pointed to the long and colorful lines of Indians walking the mile toward the prison barricade. Banners, flags, and colors shone in the afternoon sun, and then the singing and chanting and drums surrounded us.

One of the prison directors, Mr. Boon, was smoking a black curved pipe. He stepped past the iron gate. He moved fearlessly among the Indian medicine men and chiefs, and asked to speak to the leader. White Fox snapped his picture.

Ernie Peters and Greg Zephier moved forward to speak. Mr. Boon offered the Indians a deal. If they would present the names of five men who wanted to see Peltier, prison officials would select two out of the five to be allowed inside. Mr. Peters and Mr. Zephier conferred. They selected themselves, John Trudell, Clyde Bellecourt, and David Hill. The official called in the names to the command post inside the prison, to the FBI.

Ernie Peters and John Trudell were selected. They came forward and stood near the iron barricade painted yellow with black stripes. Mr. Peters held out Leonard's red stone pipe, took out the wooden stem, and showed Mr. Boon the red willow bark tobacco. He told Mr. Boon that Leonard Peltier's pipe is an important part of his religion.

The white man inspected the pipe with interest. His own curved pipe moved as he chomped the stem. Four hundred Indians watched as the two men negotiated, separated from each other by the government's yellow striped steel pipe. Mr. Boon gently explained that prison code restricts <u>anything</u> from being carried into the prison from the outside. He may bend or even break the law if he allowed Ernie Peters to enter the top security prison carrying the pipe. I could appreciate the official's position. A few years back I was thrown out of that same prison and a fat union job too, when I tipped a waiter a quarter. The painting foreman told me they had good lunches in the prison cafeteria for only a dollar. The men serving the tables looked a little crafty, perhaps, and I should have guessed they were serving time and were not hired locals. I tipped the waiter and thought nothing more about it, but shortly after I started back to work, the guard who escorted us inside the prison showed me a printed form that said, "All materials sent to or received from an inmate not authorized herein, or by Bureau policy, shall constitute contraband within the meaning of 18 U.S.C. 1791, which provides a sentence of up to 10 years. This includes the introduction into, or taking from, any correctional institution <u>anything whatsoever</u> contrary to any rule or regulation." I told the guard I wasn't going to sign that paper, and I didn't know I was doing anything wrong at the time. He told me he may lose his transfer and a promotion too. All because of the "clean" sandwich copper-centered quarter, worth all of sixteen cents, that I'd left beside my plate in the prison cafeteria.

I lost my job.

Paul Boon kept his job and refused Leonard's sacred pipe permission to enter the prison. Ernie Peters untied a soft deerskin bag from his belt and handed it and Leonard's pipe to the carrier behind him.

Mr. Boon should have known he was depriving a Native American of his Freedom of religion. Incarcerated Catholics had their rosary beads. Why deny the Redman the prayers of his sacred pipe, the symbol of traditional Indian belief?

Leonard Peltier's sacred pipe was placed on the altar with the stem pointing toward the prison. Ernie Peters, John Trudell, and the Associated Press guy were driven toward the prison in an army-green station wagon. The rest of us four hundred people were told to leave. A few women and children gathered wild onions growing in the spring grass along the shoulders of the road back to the Grange Hall Free Will Baptist Church. Four warriors stayed on the spot to guard and protect the altar and Leonard's pipe, which was to remain for three days and nights. A tent was set up and the guard was constant, as was the entrance to the prison.

Iron Moccasin and several other Indians were locked up inside Marion Federal Pen, but I couldn't figure out why such a big deal was being made of Leonard Peltier. I couldn't have know that Leonard's case history is by far the largest successful cover-up of some of our government's deepest corruption. The FBI coerced witnesses, produced false evidence, suppressed ballistics, influenced the judge, controlled the location of the trial, dictated which lines of defense could not be used, kept the defense testimony from the jury to insure a guilty verdict, and then, in prison, tried to bribe an assassin (Standing Deer) to kill Leonard, let Leonard be moved to a minimum security prison instead of the escape-proof Marion, let Leonard escape in order to justify assassination, shot Dallas Thundershield in the back, hung the poet Bobby Garcia who was involved in the escape, helped Rocky Duenus who was also involved disappear, upon appeals coerced 2 of the 3 judges and then graduated Billy Webster clean out of the 8th circuit to head the FBI, which was also able to smash our "free" press (LA Times and others), and tried to hold up The Spirit of Crazy Horse through lawsuits and threats to Peter Matthieson and his publisher.

STATE OF ILLINOIS)
              ss.
COUNTY OF JACKSON)

AFFIDAVIT

____DAVID HILL, being first duly sworn upon oath deposes and states as follows:

    1. My name is David Hill. I am currently the coordinator for a Spiritual Quest of approximately 250 Indian people walking from California to Washington DC, to bring attention to some eleven bills of anti-Indian legislation now pending in Washington DC as

well as attempt to bring about a rebirth of spirituality and brotherhood in America.

2. On May the fifteenth I waited all day at the federal building in East St. Louis in an attempt to testify as to the need for Leonard Peltier to have personal audience and ceremony with our holy men.

3. Had I been allowed to testify, my testimony would have been:

> 1. Leonard Peltier is a Sun Dancer and Carrier of the Sacred Pipe. This is a very great Honor with the Great Spirit as well as with our people.
> 2. To be a pipe carrier is a very great responsibility.
> 3. To be a Sun Dancer is an even greater responsibility.
> 4. The sacred pipe was given to Indian people a long time ago, by a sacred person

from the spirit world. It is to be used to worship within prayer.

The Great Spirit has told our people that when we pray with the sacred pipe we should do so in all honesty. We should pray and smoke the sacred pipe in council and brotherhood. When we place the stem of the sacred pipe to the bowl it is a prayer in itself, a prayer of unity with our brothers and all creation and most of all in a covenant with our creator. As our breath mingles with the smoke of the sacred tobacco it also mingles with all creation as our prayers go out to the Great Spirit and become much stronger, for then we are praying in unity and brotherhood.

The sacred pipe is used in the sacred Sun Dance.

Our people pray and fast for four days and nights when they Sun Dance.

On the fourth day the dancers are pierced and tied to the sacred tree of life which is at the center of our circle of life and in sacrifice at the day's end must pull loose, thus giving one's own self and one's own blood for our people.

In this way we are an integral part of our people's spirituality and they are part of ours.

It is very important for Leonard to share his dreams and visions with his elders, our holy men, and most important they smoke the sacred pipe together.

The vow of the Sun Dance is for four consecutive years. Leonard's Sun Dance vow has been interrupted, making his smoking of the sacred pipe with our holy men more important.

Our people have come a long way carrying a sacred pipe. Leonard's sacred Sun Dance pipe. We are poor people and can't afford to come here often.

We sincerely ask that you allow Leonard to be visited by our holy men.

I feel very inadequate in speaking of things so sacred, but for our brother Leonard I have tried my best and yet limit my writings. The road of life for an Indian person practicing his traditional beliefs and spirituality as ever teaching and unending and is sometimes referred to as "The Longest Walk."

I am American Indian.
I am a pipe carrier.
I am a Sun Dancer
I have spoken the truth.

May we all live in harmony with the Great Spirit, the Mother Earth, our fellow men, and respect our brother's vision.
Sincerely,

David Hill (CHOCTAW)

Signed and sworn before
me this 16th day of May 1978
    Claudia K. Cummins   .Notary Public

Leonard Peltier's sacred pipe was placed on the altar with the stem pointing toward the prison . When Ernie Peters and John Trudell were driven toward the prison in an army green station wagon, Charlie Roberts, the AP guy had a front seat for all the inside action, while I found myself sitting on the front steps of the Free Will Baptist Church surrounded by Indians and Buddhists. A beautiful woman with long black hair changed her baby on the hood of a red station wagon. A white man not with the Indians handed out a Communist newspaper from Chicago, which contained violent pictures.

"Has it got anything about Indians in it?" he was asked.

"No, I don't think so. Not this issue," he replied.

The young Indian threw it on the ground. Others stuck them in their pockets, maybe to start cook fires later. No one seemed interested enough to do more than glance at a couple of pictures. I wondered who was paying for this balding radical so obviously not with the Indians. How did he know the Indians were coming without any public mention in Chicago? Mild Cointelpro tactics.

Finally there was room for me in the back of a pickup protected by a camper shell. Inside sat a worn-out teenage couple snuggling in a corner, one Buddhist monk, two girls aged ten and eight, and a soft-spoken Sioux woman from Minnesota.

"This is one of the proudest moments I've had," said the woman. "One of the few times in history." She had risked her job with an Indian agency to come. The Longest Walk had been dubbed an AIM event or a communist-socialist event by her superiors, who urged that no Indians employed by the government should attend. She supported two kids, she said, and had to be there because she felt strongly that the passage of anti-Indian legislation would have a devastating effect on the Native American land base and freedoms of worship and sovereignty. "We're trying to hang on to something we don't want to lose," she said, as the pickup moved toward the campground at Ferne Clyffe.

The children encouraged the monk sitting across from them in the bed of the truck to play his *fan tieko*. He refused them gently, with smiles.

"Play it. Okay? Play it and sing 'Namo moho regge ko.'" She had picked up the sounds and rhythms of the Lotus Sutra, but not the words. I don't think the Great Mystery minded.

One of the little girls passed her hand through her thick hair, and then giggled with her girlfriend about the shaved head of the monk sitting beside her. They both laughed at him. He absorbed the abuse with genuine smiles. He offered the prayer drum to them, saying, "You pray. You pray." Did he mean "play"?

The older girl played Indian rhythms on the *fan tieko*, singing something in her own language. We neared Ferne Clyffe State Park.

While we had been gone the Indians set up two tents at the iron gate blocking the gravel road leading to the main campgrounds. Indian security guards with dogs and two-way radios stood at the gates accepting the donated steaks, clothing, and money from curious whites, but they let very few outsiders in to the campsite. The heavies had arrived-- the holy men, the PR men, and great chiefs from many tribes who had traveled from all over North America to support Leonard Peltier.

Back in camp the Buddhist monk with whom we had traveled rejoined his brother monks with clasped hands and polite bows. The fat young lamb donated by the United Church of Christ chewed grass peacefully next to my camper. The Indians were taking down the tipi they had erected under the headlights the night before. I was sad to see it go so soon.

A small dog ran near the central cooking area, sniffing around for scraps. There was a steaming iron kettle of soup cooking over the fire, seasoned with fresh-picked wild onions. The dog and the soup reminded me of the previous Sunday, when I had called the Carbondale phone number on the Longest Walk flyer, and had been invited by the lawyer Jeff Weiss to a meeting at his home. He said an Indian would be there.

We sat cross-legged on the floor of his living room. A hyperactive poodle hopped all around and onto peoples' laps and ran through the papers scattered on the floor. Jeff Weiss was upset, not at the poodle, but at having been denied access to Leonard Peltier. He said that the prison officials had taken away Leonard's books and papers. Briefs were written later that night to be presented in an East St. Louis courtroom the following morning. Weiss asked David Hill, TLW representative, to try to explain in writing what the pipe meant to the traditional Indian for the court statement. It was past eleven, but David Hill, who had been driving all day, said he would do the best he could.

We talked a bit first. David Hill said that the Southwest Indians would like the lamb, but that the Sioux were not mutton eaters. "You know some Indians eat dog?" he said. "Their *favorite* is poodle."

"Oh my God!" said a young woman who was present, putting her hand to her mouth in horror.

"Then if we can find a chicken to cook it with," David Hill continued, "we can make chicken-poodle soup."

It took a long while for the laughter to subside.

The dog out at Ferne Clyffe found a bone and ran off toward the bushes to gnaw on it. Regina Brave Dixon was still near the fire. I tried to fill my plastic milk jug from the automatic shut-off nozzle. I held the mouth to the spigot opening and when I shoved down on the water saving device, a blast of water came out of that one-inch pipe that was strong enough to peel the rings off a coon's tail. Water ran everywhere, curving away toward the woods in a little chlorinated river.

A young Sioux named Orville stood by watching, waiting for water. He said he was a part of the *Run For Survival*, the Indian survival school kids from over twenty-seven tribes, from Fort Snelling to Lawrence, Kansas. The runners started out two hundred strong, carrying the pipe. Many were to attend the survival school conference on July 15 in Washington. Forty of the runners finished the entire 1620 mile run. Grep Zephier, a Sioux leader, was one of the founders of the survival schools, which stress traditional values, the protection of the earth, and cultural awareness and pride. Greg Zephier told us that when the concept first began taking shape some years ago, they first set up two large tipis with a sacred staff standing between them. The teachers intended to teach the smaller children in one tipi, and the older ones in the other. Without any wind at all, the sacred staff began to move suddenly. It leaned toward one of the two large tipis set up side by side.

The medicine men fasted and prayed with the pipe. After numerous sweats, after many days, a dream came to one man. In this dream it was revealed that the children of all ages should be taught in one tipi. They, like the tribes, should not be divided. This is the way some survival schools are still taught, reminding me of the one-room country schoolhouses that, in many ways, were superior to the current educational system.

Orville told me this story about the *Run For Survival*. An Indian youth in his early twenties left the *Run*. He went off the Red path and drank. He drank and walked the streets all day, from bar to bar and back again. This went on. One night, however, the Indian youth did not fall asleep quickly, as he usually did. His feet hurt him. As he lay on the bed, hungover, his feet hurt as much as his head. He looked down at the feet stretched out before him and remembered the last time his feet had blisters on them-- when he spent days in the *Run For Survival*. His blisters they were for the people. Now his head hurt as badly as his feet but he had nothing to show for it. Nothing. The Indian youth returned to the *Run*, to The Longest Walk, where alcohol was prohibited, and walked the rest of the way to Washington, DC, for his people.

The Indians never wasted a tree. Only dead and fallen logs fueled the fires that cooked the food, chased the chill of early dawn, and heated the sweats, which looked like little canvas-backed turtles. Roaring fires of thigh-sized logs turned the stones for the sweats red hot. The sweats continued, as the fire did, for three days and nights.

Four braves continued to guard the sacred altar before the prison gate. There were stories in front of campfires, four men playing the same drum, ancient rhythms, newer songs, the AIM song, The Longest Walk song. I moved from camp to camp among the different tribes, hoping to be a volunteer goodwill ambassador from Southern Illinois. I was offered coffee and told stories. I was made to feel welcome by most of the Indians.

The sky tried to clear. The new moon looked like a clipped fingernail slipping in and out of the shifting cloud cover. Stars shone clear above the big white tipi, which had been moved to a grassy meadow away from the noise of the main camp. Young cedar trees rose as shadows scattered over the meadow among the tall grasses. The large fire silhouetted the Indians as they moved about looking after coffee, bush tea, and barbecue.

That night a lovely woman caught "the rooster". A new voice called the camp awake while the rooster slept in. The Buddhists chanted and played their prayer drums to the rising sun. Sometimes during the day they played moving in a straight line, six monks in orange robes, single file. They passed by a red Apache pickup, as easy to count as sheep jumping up a loading ramp, one by one.

The rooster finally woke up. He and the other camp criers called everyone to a mass meeting by the central cooking area. It was Wednesday, the 17th of May, the day scheduled for workshops. We all met by the truck and U-haul that carried the bulk of the Walk's bedding and provisions. At the beginning of the meeting, each group that had just joined was asked to give an account of the numbers in their caravan, and the tribes represented.

Louise Kitchpeme, a Menomonee from Wisconsin, a frail old woman, claimed that many Indians were in a "dictatorship of work." "We would lose our jobs if we took more than one day off," she said. "I was there every day of Leonard's trial. 'Glad to see you, Louise,' he would tell me. I have a heart condition. I am very sick, but I am here in support of our brother."

The Indians yipped, hundreds of them. The old woman sat down and a young man stood up. "I am Michael Denny. I quit my job and hitchhiked all the way to the Walk. I often slept along the roadside." Again there was applause and hoots from the crowd.

Dozens of new arrivals spoke of their individual caravans and tribes. Someone said there would be a benefit concert on the 23rd of July at the RFK stadium in Washington, the home of the Redskins. There was to be camping near the reflecting pools, with West Potomac Park to handle the overflow from the expected thousands of Indians pitching their tents on the White House lawn. The sweat lodge was to be in a wooded place fifteen miles outside the park. A place, he said, with unpolluted water.

He also said that the AIM appeals had succeeded, through the Freedom of Information Act, in obtaining 80,000 pages, or 60 volumes, of information, available for ten cents per page. He charged that the price was prohibitive, and that it was a restriction of poor peoples' right to information about themselves in government files. The man asked for readers and research people to dig for facts to help Indian causes. He told us to search for names of spies.

Another man stood up and said that many of the support vehicles were old, and that there was not enough money for gas and parts.

Volunteer sheets went around. I signed up for the PR workshop, intending to write a little feature story about my small part of The Longest Walk, which might result in some letters to senators, if my writing was sharp enough. I couldn't have known that the PR was the "think tank" for the united Indian nations, and that I was already a suspected spy.

The head of security, a man named Sunny, said he needed more trained volunteers for crowd control. He estimated that he would need five hundred security personnel by the time the group reached Washington, when the number of Indians and sympathizers would number into the thousands.

Chief Crow Dog spoke. He said that he wanted no litterers or loafers. No job was to be considered too small-- carrying wood, cooking, security, or PR. Every job was equally important, he said, to make The Longest Walk a success.

Steve Robideaux, AIM leader, stood up and spoke about his caravan's arrival from Washington State. "When it's time for the geese to go south," he said, "they don't argue over who's going to be the leader. They just get up and go!" Hoots and shouts of agreement followed.

Rumor had it that a couple of hundred Indians stomped on some strawberry plants at the Free Will Baptist Church yesterday, maybe those who were foraging for wild onions. We would no longer be permitted to park on Christian ground. Ernie Peters issued a Strawberry Statement that went something like this: "We don't care if we have to walk. That's what we're here for. Just don't push us too hard. And no pictures or tape recordings of our ceremonial acts will be tolerated!"

Everyone started piling into buses, cars, and vans. Matt Yellow Man sat in the open bed of a red truck surrounded by the monks. Two Indians walked with me. "Look at Yellow Man, in there with all those bald heads." They waved at Yellow Man, who grinned from ear to ear. "I think they're trying to talk him into a haircut."

I drove the old Dodge truck on the last day. The fifty car caravan stopped at a place near a camp from the *Trail of Tears*, which was the forced Indian march from Georgia to Oklahoma, in the last century.

Chief Crow Dog asked us to form a circle on a rounded hilltop. He asked if any Indians had relatives who may have been on the *Trail of Tears*. These people formed a circle within the larger circle and prayers were offered in memory of them and for the continuing strength of the Cherokee nation.

The Indians broke camp later that day, and I was left alone, driving home. I saw a state historical marker near the location of the *Trail of Tears* ceremony. It read:

Cherokee Camp
1935

During January, 1839, thousands of Cherokee Indians, en route from Georgia to Indian Territory and unable to cross the Mississippi because of floating ice, were encamped one mile north of here. Unprepared for the intense cold, nearly 2,000 of the 13,000 Indians who started lost their lives during the journey.

Erected, State of Illinois
1935

PRISON LETS TWO INDIANS VISIT
by Charles Roberts
Associated Press Writer

May 15, 1978. A group of American Indians assaulted America's most secure prison with prayers and the prison administration invited two of them inside to speak with an Indian serving life prison terms for the slaying of two FBI agents.

Indian drum beats and chanted prayers rolled through the quiet valleys surrounding the U.S. penitentiary near Marion Tuesday as the 250 Indians sought the help of the Great Spirit for Leonard Peltier.

Peltier, 33, was convicted in April of last year of slaying FBI agents Jack Coler and Ron Williams at the Pine Ridge, SD, Indian Reservation. He claims the jury relied on manufactured and circumstantial evidence.

The Indians clustered tightly on the road leading to the prison: Old men and women, Indian men in the prime of life, children and a few white supporters.

Warden George Wilkinson sent word through an assistant that two Indians could enter the prison and visit Peltier. Ernie Peters of Sisseton, SD, and John Trudell were chosen.

Trudell is spokesman for those in The Longest Walk, an Indian trek from Sacramento, Calif., to Washington.

THE GURU FOR THE INDIANS

After *East West Journal* said "I like the way you write very much," and may pay expenses, I got all inspired and flew to Newark, New Jersey and called the senior editor, Sherman Goldman, and he gave me five questions for the Most Venerable Fujii, and told me that the 93 year old Buddhist was one of Ghandi's teachers, and a highly respected man, well known in India, Japan and Sri Lanka.

My brother 'Jumping' Jack, a man named Bush and I drove to the nation's capitol in an old Ranchero, and pulled into the Greenbelt park on the 13th of July, two days before the arrival of The Longest Walk. We drove around the park looking for Indians, and finally found the Dearth Valley Shoshones clanging horseshoes over in one corner of the park already reserved for the six nations, and the Oglalas.

The Jersey boys started clinging up ringers, and the main part of The Walk had not yet reached the park. The Shoshone's and we three Anglos were told to leave by Lakota security, so we set up at a different part of the park and sipped a little wine they'd brought from California. The Longest Walk security came by two more times--half-way approved of our camping spot, and noticed the red wine in our paper cups. They did not smile. The sign at the gate says, "No weapons. No alcohol. No drugs. And they meant it. The main tribes were due in Washington tomorrow.

Cooking on an open fire, we ate fried potatoes and onions wrapped in tinfoil, corn on the cob and steak sandwiches, and slept deep. I cruised the camping area the next day looking for someone I knew, and saw a dull green, huge army truck dump ten cords of split white oak among the leafy green of the lush Maryland early summer.

 The bearded Bush and I slept on the ground. I piled dry leaves in plastic bags for a mattress, and Jumping Jack slept in the truck. Early the next morning, the fourteenth of July, I spoke to a group of traditional Indian women, one of whom was Wally Feather's wife. A lovely woman, small in stature with power and endurance and caution in her countenance. She wore hand beaded and silver and turquoise jewelry, armbands, belt and necklaces. I was greeted with cold suspicion at first, and then the slow warming up and beginnings of friendship were hinted, as I was slowly allowed into the conversation. I keep forgetting I am a white American who doesn't know how to mind his own business.

 I found two Japanese men, one in street clothes and one in white baggy cotton pants soiled from all the camping and open-fire cooking, a monk without his saffron robes. I mistakenly spoke to them both in front of the Indian woman. I showed the two Japanese a copy of *East West Journal*, and Sherman Goldman's letter, and slowly managed to ask them how I could get the man they call The Most Venerable Fujii Guruji. They phoned the D.C. temple, and the interview was set up for three o'clock that afternoon, so I washed myself up in the park sink as best I could and drove one monk and myself into Washington and pulled behind the two story house and parked the truck out back and followed the saffron robes around to the front where a fifteen-foot-tall white granite 'monument' stood before the temple. It was four feet wide, two feet thick like a stone domino standing on the small edge and had Japanese letters carved into it, and the inside of the letters was painted gold.

 The monk took out his prayer drum, and sounded and chanted Namu Myo Ho Renge Kyo as we walked, circumambulating the monument twice, stopping four times with fingers and palms together bowing a little from the waist and I followed him around like a chick followed her hen, and reminded myself to try and be humble. The East West editor told me that Ven. Fujii was a very humble man, and I reminded myself to try and be likewise, as much as a double Leo from Hackensack can be. I took off my shoes and left them outside the front door like everyone else.

I was served sugarless green tea in a handmade bowl sitting on the floor before a low table. I was glad I had on clean socks, and waited a half hour, and then was summoned by the leaders interpreter upstairs and into the room where the Most Venerable sat in full lotus position, legs and feet covered in red gold robes; only his bald head and folded hands could be seen. Two orange pillows were between him and the floor. There were six or seven of his monks sitting around us, and one man placed a cushion on the floor for me to sit on across a foot thick low four foot round wooden redwood burl directly across from Gurujii. I took out my 'deep' questions from Sherman Goldman and tried to write down the answers as fast as the interpreter could repeat the patriarch's words in English. To his left was an altar with a packet of rice, yellow flowers, bronze incense burners, a statue of the Buddha, a photograph of Dennis Banks and a Sri Lankan peace pagoda, and to his right is a narrow bed and on a fireplace mantle were sacred objects, eagles wing fan, and symbolic beaded medicine bag containing a sacred pipe of the Indian people given in appreciation of his great contribution to The Longest Walk: To its unity. Its non-violence prayed for daily by his monks.

A.P. The Indian leaders and security people think I'm a spy. They don't want me in camp.

Ven. Fuijii This is a question difficult to say what to do, but you must show your sincerity and walk together with the people. This is what the leaders are also wishing, not only Indians, but the black people and the white people to walk together. This is why we are walking. Since among the white people, some of them tried to do various wrongs and some of them tried to break down The Walk from the inside. These people were driven away from The Walk. So this is the reason why the security become very cautious. Despite this, if you want to show your sincerity and if you have a sincere heart you must bear and bear and endure and take part in this walk. For the success of The Longest Walk. Tomorrow will be the only day for walking, but if you want to join The Walk, and want to join as a white person, why not join the Japanese people and walk with them? The Indian people have trusted us tried to break down The Walk from the inside. So join us and take part in The Walk. I will recommend you to the Indian people.

The honorable Fujii then gave me a new copy of the wrinkled up trail worn picture book about Sri lanka, I first saw in Ferncliff Park, Marion Illinois. Please sign it for me, and handed him a red pen. He slowly wrote on the inside cover in ancient Japanese calligraphy, a quotation from The Lotus Sutra. "To wear the armor of Ninniku, which means to bear or to endure. He went on. "When you are trying to disseminate Buddhism you will be confronted by various hardships, but you will be frequently disgraced. In order to protect your heart from being hurt and protect it no matter what may come from the outside, you wear this armor of Nikkinu. Not too many white people have truly devoted themselves to the Indian people. So I hope you will become the first white person who will truly work for the sake of the Indian people. Devote your whole self to the Indian people."

"It's the lowest thing a person can do is to gain money from others and to earn money. If a person leads a life of working and taking money from people--, but if you want to join the walk for peace, you must stay outside and feel the people and nature. In order for the world to change peacefully first the two nations of the world, The United States and Russia must change. The change must come from black and red, and few white men must change the United States from the inside. The Indian people have to take the lead in the Peace revolution of The U.S. The Indian people have a long tradition of prayer and religious belief and a way of life that is completely different from the way of life of the rest of civilization. I will be leaving the United States. Nothing is to be regretted. I am happy for the Indian people."

The interview took an hour and a half, and a monk told me later that I was a lucky man for being allowed so much time with Fujii Guruji and he had a ticket to Japan waiting for me at the San Francisco temple. I cried. Trying to get myself 'together' after the culture shock of the Indian camp and Buddhist prayer drums and chants, I notice a printed document form The Longest Walk in the vestibule of the temple where I was going over my notes and trying to believe that I was going to walk with the Indians and then be a guest of The Most Venerable to Japan. The document read like a poem.

"We have come to hear the prophesied of our elders, and so we are gathering in the East: our minds are of one mind, and we are carrying the pipe and the colors of the four directions: red, yellow, black, and white.

We are the spiritual rebirth of the Western Hemisphere; we are the physical evidence of the Western Hemisphere; we are the guardians of Turtle Island.

We have heard our elder's wish to speak to the four directions; we have heard the voices from the East, and they call us."

FUJII GURUJI'S MESSAGE TO THE INDIAN PEOPLE
NA MY MYO HO REN GE KYO
NA MU MYO HO REN GE KYO
NA MU MYO HO REN GE KYO

After a long walk, the walkers have finally arrived here. You will again start walking, heading towards Washington DC. During the past 200 years your ancestors have walked from east to west. However, it was a trail of tears, it was a trail of death. This time a great walk from the west has at last been initiated. This is a walk of peace. This is a walk of justice. This walk will step out a just and peaceful path for the world, for humankind, and to a smaller extent, for the United States of America.

The Longest Walk did receive much publicity or coverage here in the United States. However, it has crossed the Pacific Ocean and reached Japan. The Japanese youth decided that they must support this action, this walk, and are holding a great gathering. An Indian youth with the message of Mr. Dennis Banks has visited Japan to attend this meeting. Most major newspapers and mass media surrounded the Indian representative to cover the story of The Longest Walk and convey it to Japan.

A moral act, a spiritual activity, and an action of non-violence seems as if it is an isolated effort. However, it can be understood and shared throughout the world. The Longest Walk is not a walk only for the Indian peoples, but will be the beginnings of a walk for the sake of constructing world peace by the awakened people of the globe. Please continue walking, believing that this is not a walk only for the Indian peoples but a great walk for constructing world peace for all of humankind.

I have heard rumors that from here to Washington DC some people will run and some must remain. But in order that every single walker may reach Washington DC, I would like to extent my cooperation to the best of my ability. I would like to make this offering to the leaders of The Longest Walk.

NA MU MYO HO REN GE KYO
NA MU MYO HO REN GE KYO
NA MU MYO HO REN GE KYO

Translated by Yumiko Miyazaki

OH DEAR, THE POOR SQUIRREL!

Don't even ask me what I was doing out at night, deer hunting out of season on restricted grounds with the wrong kind of gun and a drunk rebel called River Rat for a guide and driver.

He drove up to Indian Creek Farm in his hot '55 Chevy, complete with Corvette engine, one hell of a hotrod for a father of six to be double-clutching and riding down into the ruts, speed-shifting over washouts and foaming up the case of Falstaff half quarts in the back seat. Most people stop where the road turns bad, but I got the definite feeling that River Rat sometimes did things just to see if he could get away with it. Like a lean and wild teenager, he had petrified into a kind of playful and permanent rebellion that prescribed a rougher than average, though seldom dull, path for him to trod.

After he'd popped the tops off nearly half the case, he wanted to show me how his Chevy would run. Parked, it looked like it was running downhill all the while. Purple metallic, with white vinyl interior soiled by greasy pants. Miles of backroad gravel dust dulled its shine. Inside at night the spotlight handle reflected chrome green with the color of the dash lights.

The engine sounded like it wanted to run, and the 90 mile-an-hour ride out past Murphysboro was nothing. We pulled into a country bar parking lot heavy with dusty pickups-- old clunks. After we helped close the bar, we drove down the highway, turning off on a back road. Soon distant farmhouses became scarce. He turned up a gravel road curving along the steep bank of the levees protecting the rich bottom lands from flooding. Government lands. River Rat killed the motor and lights, took his .22 single-shot from the truck and plugged the spotlight into the cigarette lighter. We drove slowly along the top of the levee with the lights off.

The Mississippi churned and whispered with the cottonwoods on one side, and tasseled corn on the other. You could barely make out the neat rows in the new moon. The blast of a barge air-horn busted up the silence and upstaged the whippoorwills. The steady throb of diesel power moved on by us. Tug lights sent red streaks running across the broad and shifting face of the great river.

I began to wonder what I was doing out there, when River Rat held his hand up for silence. The sharp beam of the spot funneled out into the darkened levee bottom, and caught one eye glowing red like the tug light on the river. The gun steadied on the dusty car hood. The .22 popped once, the light went out, and the thumping we heard was not from my chest, as I first thought, but from the beating wings of a helicopter moving in fast from not so high above the sandstone bluffs rising beyond the corn fields.

The helicopter spotlight made River Rat's light look like a kerosene lamp, and he hollered, "Open the trunk!" throwing me the keys and running down the levee bank in great steps, reaching the fallen deer in the dark.

He usually field-dressed his kill leisurely sipping his beer. Not this time. Now he came uphill in a heavy-footed lope, grunting under 125 pounds deadweight thrown over his shoulders. The antlers bobbed as he stepped, and he dropped the carcass in the trunk and swung in behind the wheel. The blades of the copter beat the air so loud that I couldn't hear the roar of the Corvette as we spun gravel and grass out behind us, leaving the chopper spotlight shining on tire-burned gravel, and we were gone. Hunted.

The spotlight followed us and the pilot spun the aircraft around. River Rat popped second gear, saying, "Hook your seat belt, neighbor. I can't be feeding five hundred dollars to no government!" The top of the levee behind us flashed red with the sheriff and game warden moving in, now that they thought they had the River Rat cornered. The levee road had no other access, but he double clutched into first, and slid off the levee at a 45-degree angle, mudgrips churning sod and chewing up grass behind us. I held on to the door handle to keep from being thrown toward the driver, and only the intense forward motion kept us from turning over. He never touched the brake-- into second my head snapped back as we crossed a field access road, running beneath overhanging trees and honeysuckle smelling sweet in the night air.

    We sat silent in the cover like hunted foxes 'til the heat passed by and over us, the beating of wings finally growing weaker, followed by the sheriff, spotlight swinging from side to side trying to see where we'd left the levee road.

    "Sweet stolen meat, you'll get the best of me yet!" said River Rat, now running in and out back of Grand Tower alleys 'til the '55 Chevy was safely parked under a friend's shed. The deer was quartered, wrapped, and into the freezer by the time the game warden got River Rat's wife out of bed.

    "He's been out of town working on some bridge up by Chester," she said, pulling her robe about her. Two dark-eyed kids stared blankly at the lawmen 'til the big men began to shift from one foot to the other. They excused themselves and left, knowing full well that they were at the right place. They also knew River Rat was feeding six kids and trying to party a little now and then. The sheriff didn't look as hard as he could have, since the game warden poaches a little himself on the side. What could he say? Or it could have been the hunter's sense of fair play, something all good hunters are obsessed with-- when the fox reaches his burrow, when he deer disappears, when the coon dogs run out of scent, when the rabbit's in his tunnel, or when the squirrel is safely in his hole in the white oak tree, the hunt is officially over. The hunted won that round.

    "Gran-Tar," which was how one pronounces what looks like "Grand Tower," was still a little hot, so River Rat took his brother-in-law's old pickup and we drove through Pine Hills recreation area. Tall sandstone bluffs cast long crisp shadows across the early day. We pulled over to a deserted camp area. I started the fire, and soon the venison steaks simmered over hickory coals, sending white smoke up into the treetops to chase mosquitoes as it rose. For a while the poptops flew, and the River Rat finally lay sprawled on the hard wooden bench, sleeping like a baby, snoring like a man.

He woke when the food was ready and said right off, "Did you see the old lady's face light up when that deer hit the freezer? She's part Indian. The quickest way to sweeten her mouth is fresh venison. It's her favorite. Wait 'til I git home! Whooey, will she take care of me!" River Rat drifted silently into fantasy.

"Don't you feel bad about poaching?" I asked, chewing.

"Nope. You won't catch me out there with all those Chicago gunmen and their fancy automatics. Bam- Bam- Bam- Bam! No sirree, I'll be laying low with the smartest of the deer that weekend, you can be sure of that!"

"If everybody thought that way, there wouldn't be any deer left," I said.

"There's more deer now than there ever were around here. My granda settled here. Said in those days you couldn't hardly find a deer no place. Indians killed them off is what he said. Does as well as bucks, for the hides to make fancy coats. Ever use a bow?"

"Had archery in high school," I boasted.

"Good. Here's a fine target bow you ought to be able to handle," he said, moving toward the car.

When River Rat dropped me off at Indian Creek Farm, he left me with this bow he'd traded for a beagle pup, and told me to try my luck at a deer stand in a tree. I'm not that crazy about meat, or killing either, for that matter, but I figured what the hell, why not? Didn't have nothing else to do. Besides, if any deer is ignorant enough to walk under me, and if I, who had trouble hitting a bale of hay at 50 feet, could with buck-fever-fingers manage to "harvest" him with a thin piece of wood thrust by a string, it served him right to die for being so dumb and unlucky. Strengthens the herd, a Darwinist might say.

I never gave a thought about what I would do with the head and feet, hide, black shiny hooves and white tail. Money was scarce just then, but I bought two razor-tipped wooden hunting arrows for four dollars apiece and found myself standing in a treetop eighteen feet in the air, watching the morning star slowly fade from the sky. I remembered many Indian people believe the star represents wisdom, or something, because it stands between night and day, but I could never figure out why.

Bobwhites whistled the day awake, the treetop shook with my trembling, and for six days straight, I climbed in the dark, struggling with the long unwieldy bow, getting hung up on twigs, feet slipping on the bark. I stood as still as I could once in place, and still had no sight of the wary and sly white tail deer. A squirrel scolded loudly from a treetop not twenty feet away. I'd been there so often he sort of got used to me and for some reason, his racket hit me wrong. I wanted to shoot him. Whiz, out into the woods flew a four dollar fancy-tip arrow. With me out of work, that was a pound of coffee! I never even heard it fall.

I was well vexed by now, and the second arrow sunk in the wrist-size treetop beyond the gray rascal, who turned his back to me, twitching his tail and looking around behind him to see what the sound was. All I had left was a target arrow with a smooth and rounded tip, and "Chrr, chrrrr, chrrrr," he mocked me as I released the arrow with an unfamiliar certainty. It hit him with a gentle thud high in the back leg, and he dropped from the tree like a rock and lay there shaking like me as I tried to get down too fast, nearly falling. When I dropped the bow to the leafy ground, the squirrel began to run slowly away with the arrow dragging out behind him as I hurried down my tree, wishing I had a knife to finish him off. Picking up a chunk of wood, I ran after him, feet crunching the crisp leaves. He put on speed when he heard my feet. The arrow slipped loose, and he was up an oak tree, into a hole full of acorns by the time I reached the yellow arrow with neat green feathers. The tip was blood red, and one drop held, balanced toward the earth. I don't want you to think I'm a "bleeding heart," but I would have felt worse than a rat if I'd sent a wounded deer into the forest to waste his life away, drop by drop, like that small gray squirrel.

I hoped he was going to be all right after all, but he'll probably have to walk with a limp when he reaches old age, a much wiser squirrel indeed-- at least about laughing out loud at bow-and-arrow toting humanitarians perched in treetops in the chill of early light.

PEN PALS

Red Bear, #14919-289, had no Lakota pipe inside the Marion Federal Penitentiary, the nation's top security pen, which was designed for the baddest of the bad, the meanest of the mean. Red Bear asked for help. A medicine man, or spiritual advisor, should be consulted. It might take months. My letter reminded Red Bear that patience was one of the strengths of our people. And, I added, he had a *lot* of time. He laughed and said I really know how to hurt a guy. There was a smiley face on his letter.

In August of 1988, after the sundance vows were completed, Zack Bearshield sat near the fire of the sweatlodge. We were surrounded by tall pines that sang softly with the wind, on a ridge overlooking Wounded Knee. There were no lights. The flames of the huge fire sent starlike sparks spinning in the hot air. The real stars, which the Indians called sky people, looked on quietly from their distant homes.

Soon the small sweat lodge was filled, the circle completed, and Bearshield sang the ancient songs, the four direction song, a pipesong. In the dark, in the heat and the steam and the sweat, we all prayed as hard as we could along with Zack and some other fullbloods, who prayed in the ancient language, the language of the

Lakota people. It seemed to take a long time, but the songs and prayers were strong. The four flaps were finished.

We formed a circle in the crisp night air. Wet towels hung heavy at our waists. It was quiet, and the steam rose from our bodies as we shared the sacred pipe. I waited for the right time to ask about getting a pipe inside Marion Pen for Red Bear and the other Indians to pray with. It is always proper to consult a medicine man before attempting to help with any of the old traditions. Otherwise someone might ask, "Who gave you permission?" and if there is not a satisfactory answer, trouble will follow, sure as thunder follows lightning. Or is it the other way around?

Bearshield's interpreter was told about the letter sent to me from the prison, and he shouted the words out in the quiet night air for all to hear. Zack, growing older, is a little hard of hearing. The reply came in Lakota, which went right over my head and up to the stars. The translation was that he could not give a pipe to be kept inside the penitentiary. He said that I could bring into the pen the pipe that my dad, Phillip Brings Him Back, gave me when I was adopted as a son. His instructions were that the pipe should be rubbed down with sage if handled by any guards or police. The pipe should then be protected and taken care of in the proper manner, after taking it out of the prison.

Niles Beherens, the chaplain at the Marion Federal Penitentiary, is a kind man. And understanding. He seems to be able to respect the visions and the beliefs of others, not matter how far they may be from his own. Chaplain Beherens told me about a sweatlodge already in the yard at the pen, and said that the men in honor unit B were allowed to participate in sweatlodge ceremonies once a month, if there is someone to help run the sweat. He said that I would have to fill out six pages of forms, FBI information request forms, references, criminal record forms, fingerprint card, and a regular application for employment. All the security checks of anyone wanting to contact visits with the men would apply to me.

What I was trying to do was to see that Red Bear, a full-blooded Lakota, had a traditional pipe to pray with. That he and other Indians be allowed the same rights as the Christians,

Muslims, Jews, and Rastafarians. And that he be able to pray in the way that his ancient culture, his heart, and his ancestors told him.

It was visiting day, and I was filling out forms and more forms. An elderly couple, neatly dressed, polite, kind wrinkles covering their faces, were there to visit a relative. The old man had just passed through a beeping metal detector, and stood in his stocking feet, taking off his belt. The guard at the desk asked for his pen and pencils. The old man was patient, and after he put his shoes and belt back on, his photo was snapped, and he and his wife were finally buzzed through the first of three sliding iron gates. They shuffled down the shiny tiled floor toward the visiting rooms.

"Are those people going in for a contact visit?" I asked.

"No," said the guard. "They will have to speak through a phone and be separated by thick glass. No contact visits are allowed at Marion. We've had problems with contraband."

I was amazed at the degree of security involved, just to speak on a phone, behind glass. I thought that I would never be allowed to see Red Bear. My qualifications were limited. Sure, I held the sacred pipe my dad gave me, but I was a four-quarters white guy with no Indian blood. I was not a medicine man, and could never hope to be one.

I was not a Sundancer at the time, either. All I had was the pipe and ten years' experience of traditional ways and ceremonies. I was asked to be firekeeper at several Sundances, and I had been in numerous sweats run by different medicine men, but how could I hope to be let into the nation's top security pen, when so few people are let in for any reason?

At the time, I did not consider that the prison system had been sued (siouxed?) several times by skins wanting the same rights as the whites and blacks. Praying together and sweating had only recently been allowed, thanks to the efforts of Chaplain Beherens. There was a sweatlodge out in the yard, and a Choctaw elder had been brought in every three months from Memphis to help with the sweats and prayers. I suppose the pen was required by law or regulation to provide some kind of religion for the Indians, to show fairness. Or at least to prevent further lawsuits.

Many of these problems started with Leonard Peltier, the activist, who was an inmate raised with so many questions and caused so much trouble about wanting to use a sweatlodge at

Marion that the warden was probably very happy to see him leave for another prison. Those who know Leonard say his ways are gentle and non-violent, but sometimes a quiet but determined man can still make many waves of publicity. With hundreds of Indian protesters outside the gates of the pen in 1978 and 1981, Leonard became a threat to the smooth running of the place.

Now, please understand that I am not a bleeding heart in the matter of security. I know that several guards and even more prisoners have been killed at Marion Federal Penitentiary. The potential for death and violence is always there.

But here I was, a white guy attempting to help with a traditional religion, and not sure of my acceptance by either the administration or the inmates. I thought the skins might just tell me to keep on walking and not come back. I was determined to try, however, because I was asked. It is an honor to be asked. And too, no one else was doing it--I was the closest person to the pen with any kind of direct knowledge of the ancient beliefs of these people, who were, after all, supposed to have disappeared or assimilated, but who never quite did.

Senator Paul Simon is from my little township of Makanda, in Southern Illinois. We had some dealings when he was a congressman, and when a controversy about religious freedom at the Marion pen arose once before, he had asked me for some information, admitting that he did not know anything at all about Indian religion. I had sent him a letter outlining a little of what I knew, and then, when years later he moved to the Senate, he still remembered me. He was kind enough to send a letter to the warden on my behalf, and I'm sure that helped.

In November of 1989, I was in the mountains of Jamaica, delivering 200 pounds of food and clothes to my friends there, who were suffering the effects of Hurricane Hugo. I planned to stay for two weeks. For reasons I could not say, I left early, taking the first flight out of Montego Bay. When I called home from the Atlanta airport, my wife told me that Chaplain Beherens had called to say they were having a sweat ceremony the following Saturday, and he wondered if I could make it.

On the appointed day, I grabbed my towel and pipe and headed out the back roads to the penitentiary. When I reached the speaker, they called me from the watchtower and asked what I wanted. I asked for the chaplain and was told to wait in the lobby.

"What are you doing here?" Chaplain Beherens asked. He looked like he saw a ghost. "Your wife said you were in Jamaica!"

"I was," I said, "But something told me to come back sooner than I was supposed to." I did not tell the Chaplain I thought the something that told me to come back was the red-tailed hawk that had soared across my windshield on the way to the prison.

I had been trying to get in prison for months, but by this time I felt a kind of confidence and certainty. In an hour or so I was taking off my belt, clearing the metal detector, and filling out the contraband form. They took my picture and I was escorted down the long halls to the chaplains' offices.

We began loading green army tarps onto a laundry cart, and the chaplain checked out a shovel. We rolled all this stuff down the east corridor toward the exercise yard. Four men from B unit walked through the metal detectors, were casually searched, and a guard with a radio escorted all of us out into the fenced yard.

Two skins--a Lakota named Hawk and an Apache named Jackson--and two Mexican brothers and I cleaned out the fire pit, and I loaded the pipe. After we had the fire blasting we had to go inside and wait for the two hours it would take to get the rocks red.

I had noticed right away that the sweatlodge was built so that the door faced the east and the firepit faced the west, which was the opposite of all the Lakota sweatlodges I had been around, but I didn't think much about it. I felt honored again when Jackson asked me to run the sweat. Red Bear was not able to participate because he wasn't in B unit, and Jackson had just met me. He didn't know any of the songs. I ran the sweat for him and Hawk, and it was strong and hot, and for awhile in the dark, sweating hard and praying harder, I forgot that I was inside the prison yard. When the doorkeeper flipped open the flap, I was surprised to see the rolls of razor wire shining like thousands of diamonds in the early afternoon sun.

The men thanked me for helping them out. I had made it clear from the beginning that I was not medicine man and that I had no pretense of being one-sixteenth Cherokee, or any other claim to Indianness besides my adoption by an elder. There was a little suspicion, as I expected; a holding back of friendship for a while. Then the men got to know and trust me better, and they started joshing and joking like Indians do when they are happy and comfortable with someone. We ended the ceremony with the pipe and everyone was feeling relaxed and mellow and much lighter than when we had before we went in.

A day or two later a dream came to me, in which the sweatlodge inside the penitentiary was quite clear. It had been built with too few willow poles, according to my dream, and the flimsy frame was too weak to support the covers. I dreamt that while we were inside, the walls were trying to fall in toward the center, and we had to hold it up with our hands while trying to pray at the same time. I called Archie Fire Lame Deer, who is active in prison issues, to discuss the dream with him. Archie told me to build a new sweatlodge. He had taught me how to do it years before.

I called Chaplain Beherens and explained to him that in Indian spiritual ways, dreams are most important. I mentioned that a spiritual advisor said I should build a new sweatlodge, one facing west as i should be, according to Lakota ways. As before, I had made sure I had a higher authority behind me. The Indians took unkindly at anyone pushing himself forward, especially where traditional ceremonies are concerned.

Prison officials set a date a couple of weeks away, and I started looking for groves of small willows and other things i would need for the new sweatlodge. I gathered the willows, and I offered a little tobacco to the roots of the cut poles. This was an offering to Mother Earth, so that the willows to come in years ahead would be strong. It is important to give back when you take, and my action was but a very small part of a larger system of mystic values since before Columbus got lost.

I had to do all the trimming and sharpening of the ends that would go into the ground at home, because I knew they would not let me bring my machete inside the pen. Over thirty willows were tied on the roof of my wife's blue beater Comet. The willows stuck out beyond the back of the car several yards, so I tied some red strips of cloth at the ends, put a dozen large rocks in the trunk, and headed east toward Marion.

The guard in the tower may have been surprised at the little blue car with the long poles on top, but at the speaker I mentioned that Chaplain Beherens was expecting me. I asked the guard if I could stop in front of the administration building to unload. When I got to the waiting room, the chaplain was there with a cart to load up the stones, and we put the long poles of freshly cut willows on a laundry cart and wheeled all these things down the long, shiny-tiled hall. We waited at three electronically controlled sets of bars, and then went out into the prison yard. The B unit guys were let out to help, and we took down the old sweatlodge, keeping the small dried poles for kindling to start the new fire.

It was November and the ground was wet and muddy. We started digging the new firepit. One guy had on brand new sneakers, so he took off his shoes, the mud coming up between his toes. The men were joking about digging clear out under the fence, over fifty yards away, but it was all we could do in a couple of hours to dig a pit six feet around and three feet deep. the opening of the pit was facing the east, the opening of the new sweat would be toward the west. It had been explained to me by an elder that in the good days, before the oppression, the sweats faced east. Now, in the time of sorrow and the struggle of our people, the sweats are always facing west.

We lit the fire and piled on the rocks before starting to build the new lodge. The rocks would be red by the time the sweatlodge was finished.

Jackson, the Apache, wanted to run the first sweat, so I loaded the pipe for him. When we built the lodge, Jackson was supposed to pull the top down so it would be low and flat, but it came out kind of tall, and was shaped like a rocket nosecone aimed at the sky, Dennis Banks-style. He only asked for seven rocks to begin with, and Hawk was joking about him running a cold sweat, and how he had to sit tall to feel the heat, but still more rocks were brought in and by the third flap it was so hot that Hawk was lying down. The prayers were strong, and were offered even for the jailers. Jackson asked me to lead a sweat song, and I was glad I knew some. They all joined in the prayer songs, and when we came out our bodies were slick with sweat, and the steam was rising into the late November air.

The breeze in the open prison yard felt good and we shared some beef jerky and some oranges the guys brought out. The whole world seemed a little cleaner. All the tension, stress, hostility, and anger seemed gone for a time, and Homer Ray--or was it Tumbleweed--said that he used to pay a hundred dollars on the street to feel this good.

We smoked and passed my dad's pipe, and in Jackson's prayers he thanked Grandfather for sending in a Pipecarrier to share what he knew. I did not know then that Pipecarriers have the responsibility to teach and share knowledge and experience with those who are hungry for it. I know it now.

We all shook hands, the time being up. The jailers came for us, so we took off all the tarps, picked up the shovel and waterbucket, and walked slowly back to the gray concrete walls, feeling in balance with the world and ourselves, in the heart of Marion Federal Penitentiary.

Eventually I was able to share the pipe with Red Bear, although that was a different day and another story. A good story, too. One of our stories.

DODGING

As soon as my college days ended, so had my student deferment, and I received my army induction notice. At the time I was in training for draft evasion in Los Angeles, the land of the fruits and nuts, according to my Uncle Bill.

I was at Leo's house and I got up and walked to the open window. A white moth bounced against the screen over and over, trying to reach the light.

"Then what the hell am I going to do?" I asked.

"All's you got to do is get a haircut, a shave, and a pretty shirt, and it'll be all over in a couple of weeks."

"I don't want it saying I'm a queer on my record," I said. "Think of my mother."

"What the hell's the difference, so long as you're out of their hands?" said Leo.

"But some day I might want to teach or something, and when they look at the record--"

"--They'll see 1-Y, Physical Deferment, and so you tell them you got flat feet or a bum knee or something. They don't have to know."

"They can find out," I said.

Leo shook his head. "Like hell they can." He scratched the inside of his arm. "They can't afford to let their information out. If word got around that they turned you in to the cops or came back at you in any way, people wouldn't say nothing, and the army'd be full of junkies and queers. I went through all that paranoid crap before I did the junkie number."

I was still doing research. "How did you do it?" I asked.

Leo shrugged. "I got the notice to go in for the physical in three weeks, so I took a pin and gave myself a couple of jabs every night. When I went in I had tracks up one rope and down the other. My pits looked like a fucking dartboard. So I go through all the tests, and where it said on the paper do I have a drug habit, I put No."

"What did you tell them No for?"

Leo leaned over like maybe he was going to sell me a dirty picture or something. "Because a junkie never admits he's got a habit, that's why. And so I go through the rest of the physical, just like the other children, until I get to the table where they want to take my blood, and I tell them 'No!' 'What do you mean, No? Roll up your sleeve,' the boy with the spike says, and I tell him, 'No, you're not going to take my blood.' And he says, 'Why not?' and I tell him, 'Because I'm not going to let you,' and he says, 'Another nut. All right, upstairs and wait at the end of the green line.' And so I follow the line and sit down with a bunch of faggots and fuck-ups and wait to see the shrink. My turn comes, and he says, 'Well now, young man. What's the problem?'

"'No problem,' I say. 'I don't want them to take my blood, that's all.' And he says, looking at me close, like the chief fruit inspector, as if even he didn't believe what he was going to ask me, 'Are you afraid of the needle?' And I couldn't help smiling a little, even though I was trying to look scared." Leo was smiling again, as pleased with himself as if he were the Buddha.

"Weren't you scared?" I asked.

"Hell, no. What's to be scared of? I wasn't going in, and that was that. So I tell the doc--" Leo leaned in toward me again, pretending I was the doctor and maybe that the walls were bugged, "Look, I'm not afraid of the needle, but I can't tell you why. I don't want any trouble.' Then the shrink, he goes into this riff about how this interview is completely confidential, and that without a Supreme Court order the files are not accessible to anyone. It has to be confidential so the army can protect itself, and he convinces me, and I whisper to him, 'It's because I got holes in my arms.' Then he asked me would I please roll up my sleeves, and he looks at my arms and then at the papers I filled out, and he sees where I put 'No' where it says about drugs, and he asks me about it, and I tell him that I like to use drugs now and then, but I don't have no habit.

"And he sits there with his nose and little mustache in the papers for a minute or so, and then he asked me if I ever shot marijuana. And I say, 'Come on, doc, you know better than that,' and then he says, 'All right, what kinds of drugs do you use?' and I look at him right in the eye, like this, and tell him, real serious, 'Anything I can get my hands on. I like being high now and then and there's nothing wrong with that.'

"And then he says he wants some names, so I tell him, kind of bored, like I'm maybe naming off breakfast cereals: 'Seconal, yellow jackets, bennies, dexy, meth, boo, and a little smack now and then. But I don't fuck with any acid. I don't take nothing that would mess with my head.' And he asks me 'how do you prepare a fix?' and I tell him about melting the crystal and sterilizing the needle and waiting for the blood bubble to rise, and the whole bit.

"He's quiet for a minute, and then he asks me how often do I use heroin. I tell him just a couple of times a week, but I don't have no habit. And he tries to tell me how drugs can fuck me up. Me, and he don't know that I seen more guys fucked up behind that shit than he could ever read about. And right then my brother Davie is sitting in Synanon. But I play it dumb and say, 'But Doc, you don't understand. I like the way I am, I like to be out of my skull a little, now and then,' and he nods like maybe he thinks he understands, and he says that will be all, and I roll down my sleeve and finish the physical and go home."

Leo leaned forward and opened the box. The wood was very old and I could see cracks as thin as as hair in several places. A frog was carved into the lid, one green eye was missing. He handed me a cigarette. I wet it and lit it and brought the smoke into my lungs before giving it back to Leo.

The sound of my voice was forced as I let out as little smoke as possible while saying, "And nothing ever happened to you? They didn't tell the cops or anything?" Tff, I took in more air.

"I already told you," Leo said, like I was an idiot. "They can't get back at you or the whole goddamned army would be full of junkies. That shit's so easy to come by overseas that anyone who even smells like he plays with heavy drugs is treated <u>very</u> special. They can't take any chances."

"All right. I believe you. But it's still a damned shame that I have to lie to them when there is a real reason why I could never make it in the army," I said.

"What the hell's the difference, so long as you're out? You ought to get a letter," Leo said.

"You know a doctor?"

"I know a guy who's gay and got out like that. Why don't you go talk to him and ask who his doctor is?" Leo got up and put on a tape of Turkish music. The rest of the night moved smoothly through the droning sounds.

The next morning I found out who the doctor was and made an appointment. The office was in downtown Hollywood, one block off the strip. The waiting room was very posh, with deep-nap pea-green carpets and gold and red flecked wallpaper. There was a large, late-period Forest Lawn bathtub-marble statue of Michelangelo's David standing graceful and religious in one corner of the room, with a fig leaf stuck to his organ. I swear to God, there were two guys already waiting. Each one had a small poodle. I couldn't help grinning, which I hid behind a magazine. When I got into the office, the doctor asked me to sit down. I immediately started to tease the fingers of one hand with the fingers of the other and make little nervous gestures, partly because I was afraid he would ask me something I wouldn't be able to answer and I wouldn't get the letter, and partly because Leo had told me to keep my hands busy. The doctor's hands were immaculate and pink and looked as though they had cold sweat on them, like a corpse in a cellar. There was a huge silver ring on his pointing finger. A paisley tie fell in bright colors from his thin neck. He was dwarfed by the side walnut desk, which was completely bare except for his pink fingers folded on the edge and a pair of fat Chinese horses, standing all fake antiquey-bronzey on one corner. "Well, what is your problem, young man?" the doctor asked me.

"Well, Doctor, um, you see, I got the notice for my physical, and my lover suggested that I come in and talk with you."

"Oh, you want a letter. Is that it?" He waved a soft hand delicately in the air.

Smart man. "Yes, if you could," I said politely.

"Dr. Crandall usually handles these matters, and he's out of town," the doctor said. "Are you a patient of his?"

"No, Doctor. Actually a friend of mine gave me his name and suggested I come in and talk with him."

"We usually cover for each other. Maybe I can help you." The doctor took a small white card from the lower drawer, and a gold Cross pen from his pocket with those thin, immaculate fingers. "How old are you?"

"Twenty-five."

"When will you be twenty-six?"

"In two months."

"They almost missed you, didn't they?" The doctor's sibilant esses grated in my ears.

"Almost is not enough."

His smile was thin-lipped. "Have you ever been married?"

"Yes, but I don't know if I ought to tell them that or not."

The doctor raised his voice. "You had better damned well tell them. Don't tell them any lies or it will be all over for you. Do you understand that? They have ways of finding things out. Just tell them the truth. You don't have to lie."

"All right, Doctor," I said, thinking about Leo. There was a short pause while that last remark settled.

"Now," he continued. "When was the first time you had relations with a man?"

"It was when I was married."

"Are you living with a man now?"

"Yes."

"When was the last time you made love?"

"Last night."

"What kinds of sexual practices do you engage in?"

I scratched my neck but it didn't itch, and the plaster horses looked fat and cold on the big empty desk. When the pause became uncomfortable, I made several false starts to say something. Finally I said, "Well, you see, I usually don't talk about such things. What happens is just between Bobbie and myself, and--"

"Now you can do better than that! I can <u>almost</u> understand your embarrassment, young man, but these questions are ones you are liable to be asked at your induction, and you better be able to come up with some answers."

"All right, I'll try. He likes to be made love to, but--"

"Do you mean he likes to be fucked?" It seemed to me the doctor leered a little.

"Yes," I said, "But it's not my thing, and sometimes he can come when I do."

"That's better," the doctor said. He was more understanding than the priest was, when I'd told him that I'd French-kissed Elane, my ex-roller skating partner form Hackensack.

"Now, do you do any cocksucking?" he asked, quite matter-of-factly.

"Well, yes," I lied timidly, as if the lack of volume would soften what I had just said.

"Good. Now remember, don't be afraid of using the words when you talk to the psychiatrist. I don't want to see those bastards get you any more than you do, and you may be in for a little humiliation, but you can't let that bother you. Do you understand?"

"Yes."

"All right. Now, what can we put in that letter?" The doctor put the tip of the pen in his mouth, sensuously, thinking, and then he took it out. "You are not a patient of mine, so this will be a little difficult. I can tell them that in my opinion you are a practicing homosexual, but I don't know if that will be enough... Who was it that recommended you to this office?"

"Robert Haws," I said, naming Leo's friend.

"Bobbie Haws told you to come here?" I could tell the doctor was fond of Bobbie.

"Do you know him?"

"Let's just say that I know <u>of</u> him," he said, a little cattily. "That's good. I can say that you were recommended to me by a practicing homosexual, and in my opinion you are also a practicing homosexual. I will have the secretary type it out, and you can pick up your letter tomorrow."

I thanked the doctor and shook his hand. "Good luck," he said. His palm was a little clammy, like a frog's belly, but I could have kissed it, because he gave me not only the questions I might be asked during my physical but the answers as well. Oakland Induction Center, I thought, here I come.

I showed the letter to Leo, who thought it would work. He said I should find a nice shirt, not too pretty, and not even to try and be too nellie, just a little, you know, "sensitive." I would have to cut off my beard and long hair. I was beginning to realize the beard wasn't working worth a shit anyway, but the mustache didn't look too bad. My Hungarian grandfather had one, and I wanted to keep it.

"No!" Leo said.

He was always so damned quick with his intuitive answers. So sure of himself. "Why not?" I argued. "If I've got a letter and I am all dressed up--"

"No," Leo said, without listening to me. "No hair on your face. If those bastards ever get the slightest idea that you are playing a fag-- No hair! I'm telling you!"

"All right. I've listened to you so far. No hair. Should I mention anything about drugs?"

"Don't say nothing about nothing. Tell them only <u>one</u> thing. One thing is better than two or three things. Everything you mention besides that will make them suspect you're trying to get out, and then they start looking hard, and you don't want that. Remember, one thing. Right?"

"Right. One thing," I said. I thought that for a semi-literate window-washer, Leo had sure got around to learning a lot.

*****

For phase two I buzzed back to San Francisco in my VW van and looked up Frank and Lynn. Frank was in his late thirties, dedicated to his job and to making a position for himself where he could live comfortably and, eventually, raise a family. Sometimes I feel that is a right answer, and I am very impressed.

Sometimes not.

To have something to offer to someone you love-- what a moving phrase. How orbicular! But then, if the love's there, two people can always work and grow together, as they say, moving toward what they both want, if it exists. If I wanted to be sententious, I could say that the answer is to Keep On Working At What You Want Right Now-- never get a saddle before you've got a horse. But sententiousness is ridiculous.

On the other hand, if you have a saddle, maybe you start looking harder for the right horse. Or, again, if you desired a horse-- for Freudian reasons or something, say-- and even though just then all you can afford is-- Oh, skip it!

Frank was thin and a nellie himself, but he had had many years of therapy and liked himself fine. He was able to form "comfortable relationships" with many kinds of people, and we liked each other okay. After dinner I joked with Lynn and Frank about the army, and talked with an outrageous lisp, waving my limp wrists in the air like two faded lilies. They eventually became interested in making me pretty.

I had a long way to go, looking as scruffy as I did, with my long hair, too-sparse beard, and coarse, square-looking hands. First the beard had to go, and then I went to a hair stylist. I ordered a full treatment-- shampoo, style job, set, scalp massage. He showed me how to brush it and touch it with my fingertips until it would act exactly as it was supposed to.

Frank was a distributor for cosmetics, and he had samples of all the latest. He brought out a bowl big enough to toss a salad for six, half filled with gadgets and goos just for the fingernails. Man, I knew I was on the way to something big.

First he soaked my hands in a special solution to soften the cuticles and to open the pores. Then he had four or five special little tweezers, clippers, knives, and pusher-backers, just for the cuticles. Then there was this bad-smelling goo that was dabbed on the cuticles and around the edges of the nails, and after the cuticles were trimmed and shaped to Frank's satisfaction, he began on the nails. They were cut and shaped and filed and emery boarded. Then a special imported buffing cream was thinly applied with its own applicator, and then buffed with a device about six inches long, half an inch thick, with a natural wooden handle and a chamois rubbing surface. Then a white pencil was run under the nails to make the even, clean edges show up better.

While Frank was working on the final hand, the second one, I mean, I held the first finished masterpiece up to the light, palm away, scrutinizing the nails like the for-some-reason-naked girl in the nail polish advertising. I have to admit, I was impressed. Frank was not completely pleased, though. Two of the cuticles had pulled back from the nail, and no amount of teasing and working could make them come back to where he thought they should be, but he declared it was the best he could do. He told me to put some cold cream on my hands and to try to keep them clean and free from harm until the physical, now only two days away.

Lynn said that I had hands like a doctor. For the two days I was so aware of my hands that I was careful putting them in my pockets, lest I injure a cuticle or roughen a nail. I even thought about not throwing a stick that Laniege, my white German Shepherd, had found in the park because it was rough and dirty. This was a strange matter for me, because while all the time I knew who I was and could laugh at myself for the seriousness with which I was taking my fingernails, it bothered me to get them dirty.

Finally, Lynn, a tailor, made a pair of white pants without pocket or belt, and lined them in silk. He said I could wear them, and he also lent me his boots. They were something to see. They had cost eighty dollars wholesale in 1962, and they came up to the knee all glossy and black, Western in style, but without any decorative stitching. Just the deep, rich comfort lines in the leather. The foot part of the boot was made of kangaroo, and the texture was beautiful.

Frank had a nice light blue shirt with subtle checks on it. It was pretty but not too fancy. Except for the underwear, this completed the dress rehearsal. When I went out I was hardly recognized by people who knew me, and I was propositioned twice without going into the Tenderloin. I gently declined the offers, but went home feeling more secure than ever. Even so, there was still a lot to fear. I was not going in, no matter what.

I even had alternate plans, as well as half a dozen schemes that had worked for others. All my research was carefully tucked away in my mind, ready to be brought into action if needed. I would rehearse the plans whenever I felt unsure of myself. One of the most interesting, and one I was sure would work, was bedwetting.

If plan A failed me, a reliable source advised, save up and carefully wet the bed each night during basic training. After several days accusations will fly, but I was told never to admit for one minute that I had anything to do with it. Acting a little embarrased or loud, pleading "I didn't do it!" would also help. Those funny smelling black sheets are not on the army supply list, and there is no other reasonable way that they can deal with the problem. The men have to sleep in close quarters. Besides, pissing my way out of the army appealed to me.

After years of dread and fear, therefore, the day of confrontation came. I dressed carefully that morning, trying to fit my balls into the folded-handkerchief-size black bikini underwear that Lynn had laid out as a surprise. A dab of Dippity Do setting gel in the hair, as Frank suggested, a hint of men's cologne. Away went the mustache. And then the finishing touch -- Bright Eyes. It's a liquid that enlarges the pupils, makes the natural color stand out, and makes the eyes appear a little moist. Presto! A fairy prince.

If any draftable young men are listening, don't worry. It's not necessary to go to such extremes. Just look clean-cut and act a little sensitive. That's enough. I have a tendency to overdo everything, Just ask the women in my life.

Out of the house and onto the army bus. Over the Bay Bridge and up to the Oakland Induction Center. The building was three stories high, made out of dull brown stone. From the roof Old Glory hung limply from her pole. Standing in front of the door was a middle-aged Quaker housewife wearing an iron peace medallion around her neck.

"Please listen to me," she pleaded. "You do not have to go. No one should have to support this morally unjustifiable war." She reached out her hand to me. In it was a pamphlet on draft resistance. I wanted to take it from her, and tell her that I knew very well that I was not going to war, but just inside the door was a green man, and he was watching us through the glass. I was too paranoid even to show I noticed her. I walked past the Quaker woman like she smelled bad. Before the door closed behind me she was talking fast, with a kind of quiet fury, trying to get something to listen to her boring rap about peace.

It was twenty past six in the morning. There were ten minutes to wait, so I was directed to sit with fifty or seventy-five other yawning and blinking young men. I looked with disbelief at the clock on the wall, and then I checked out my fingernails. A-OK was what they said. There were a few intense looking faces, with long hair, mustaches, and a few beards. I wished them luck, they would need it. And several fragile looking boys who looked as if they would shatter like fine crystal when hit on the knee with the rubber mallet. I suspected they were also on the way to the 1-Y. There was a smattering of gung-ho types who laughed and joked among themselves, who would undoubtedly be the first to volunteer for anything, would go along with all they were told, and who would indeed make wonderful soldiers.

We were divided into groups of twenty-five and led to classrooms that had chairdesks in them. A green man came into the room carrying test booklets in one arm and answer sheets in the other. He said, speaking like a machine, "You are going to take an intelligence test. Please don't open the test booklets until you are told to do so, and make all your marks within the space provided on the answer sheet. For each part of the test there will be a time limit, so work quickly and carefully in the time provided. Before you begin, I want to warn you that you'd better do the best you can. Because if you fail, you will be right back here tomorrow for another test. If you fail that one also, another test, and then another until you pass. It is an easy test to pass, and no one should have any trouble."

"Mohammed Ali couldn't pass it," someone up front said, and there was some laughter. A black man added in a deep voice, "He didn't say he was the smartest, he said he was the greatest." More laughter, and then the green man said, "We're not through with him, yet. One way or the other he'll spend his time. Either in the army, or in jail. So don't try and fail this test, because it won't do you any good."

And he began to pass the tests out, saying, "Keep you answer sheets face down on the desks, and don't turn them over until I give the signal. We will now go through some sample questions," and my mind shut off. I did not hear anything he said until, "All right, begin!" I turned the paper over and did the test. We all finished and handed in the answer blanks. We were led into a large room with hundreds of men, some in army green, others in white coats talking to others and directing traffic. Lines of men moved from here to there. Some lines were in underwear, and others had on their coats, and by this time there was very little laughter to be heard anywhere. We were given a form to fill out that asked if we had any broken bones or back trouble or ulcers, or heart murmurs or TB or were we addicted to any drugs? I thought of Leo, and I put No to all of them except for a broken collar bone when I was a kid. And we were told to insert any relevant letters we may have after page three. And I did.

  We were counted into groups of thirty and filed into a corner where there were a lot of wire baskets in pigeon holes and told to take a basket and to strip down to our shorts and shoes and to put all of our clothes into the wire baskets and line up in this room which was partitioned off from the rest of the large room by opaque eight foot high glass dividers-- images of men moved beyond the glass like fish in a tank. My feet were sweaty and it was hard to get the damned beautiful black boots off, but the white silk-lined pants slid easily from my legs, gave me a small charge. Then it hit me like a falling safe. I was going to walk around all day in that goddamned black jockstrap and those big boots! When I looked down at the skimpy bikini, it surprised me, although I had worn it all morning. I had forgotten about it. And then I looked down at the knee-high boots shining expensively under the neon lights like massive black jewels against the cheap linoleum floor. Two black tubes beneath a tiny black triangle.

  As I tried unsuccessfully to get the boots back on, hopping up and down on one foot, sweating, wishing all the while that I could shrink smaller and smaller until all that remained were the big boots and the small piece of black cloth on the floor, but I kept cool as best I could. I walked into the roomful of hairy chests, sagging tits and pimply boys, trying to look natural. Most of the other guys wore baggy boxer shorts, some with a slice of pecker showing in front, and penny loafers or wing-tip shoes. I didn't know whether to stand strong or to shrink small, or to stand at ease. I snuck a glance at some of the other faces for clues, but no one would meet my glance except that one guy.

  He was blond and very tanned. The LA surfer type. He stood tall and athletic, apart from the spare tires and beer bellies which hung around most of the other guys. He wore a pair of new white jockey shorts. Beside him stood a guy with an Indian Madras spread wrapped around himself, who talked softly to a man with a sandy mustache who would later offer me a ride back to the city.

Three men in white coats came in and told us to take off our shoes and put our papers on top of our shoes. My feet were so wet with nervous sweat that they again refused to come out of the shiny black boots. I could feel the corner of every eye on me as I foolishly hopped up and down on the one foot, trying to get the boots off and not be noticed, and I was failing at both. At last the boots came off, and I put my papers on top of them and leaned back against the wall. The guy with the Madras spread took it from his shoulders and carefully folded it and put it on top of his papers. He nodded slowly as he talked to the guy next to him, and I think he was on acid. Anyway, he was bawled out for not following directions, and he acted like it hurt him to put the golden spread on the ugly linoleum tile and the papers on top of it. He said something quietly to the man next to him, and the doctor told him that he wanted it quiet. He asked the doctor if something was wrong with his ears, and he was told to leave the room and sit outside the door. He did.

They made us touch our toes and breathe deeply, and they wrapped our arms and pumped up the rubber ball, they looked in our ears and at our feet and they asked if any of us suffered from bone damage. One or two were looked at more closely, and then we had to drop our underwear, turn around, bend over, and grab one cheek in each hand to spread them apart. I was glad I wasn't one of the doctors. When we straightened up I looked around and did a double take on the surfer type. On the narrow band of pale skin which divided his bronze body was a round blue label about the size of a baseball, readable at a glance from across the room. Tattooed on his ass, the stamp read "U.S. Government Inspected Grade A." The A was in the center of the circle, and the writing was around it. Nervous as I was, I laughed out loud, until quieted by a firm glance from one of the white coats, who was probably a green man in disguise. They weren't going to pass the surfer this time, I thought, and when you leave, they will stamp your other cheek "U.S. Government Rejected 1-Y."

Up went our drawers and out we went to visit the hearing boxes. I heard all the required beeps and toots. On to the urine tester. I remembered one of the emergency pointers from my research was to stick your finger with a pin and let some of the blood into the urine, but I had my number. A couple of guys couldn't pee, sometimes it's hard to do it on command. They had to be sent to get a drink of water. The guy doing the collecting looked bored. I asked him if he applied especially for this job, and how did he like his work? He smirked and kept putting the warm paper shot glasses of pee in their proper places.

Then came the man with the spikes. That black guy knew what he was doing, but the white dude with the glasses looked like he was practicing for a dart throwing championship. He kept an missing the veins and then stabbing again. A couple of guys passed out and were carried away on stretchers to be laid out on tables and stuck there, unconscious. My turn gave me him, and I told him politely that I would wait for the other guy. He gave me a dirty look. I told the black dude that he looked like he knew what he was doing. He smiled and said, "So would you, if you had as much practice as me."

He gently slid the needle into my vein. My breath came a little short, and my whole system seemed to wait. Nothing came except my blood.

We had to sit on some benches and wait for a private consultation with an MD, which lasted two or three minutes on the average. My doctor was a tired-looking forty, and he glanced quickly through my papers. "Is there any reason why you should not be inducted into the Armed Forces of the United States?" he asked sternly.

"Yes," I answered softly. "Because I'm gay."

He looked through the papers again and pulled out the letter. He read it carefully and then asked, "Why did Doctor Madson sign the letter on Doctor Crandall's stationery?"

"Because Doctor Crandall was on vacation that week."

He seemed satisfied with my answer. I remembered that Leo told me army doctors will seldom question a letter from another doctor unless they have specific reasons for doubt, because, after all, what can you find out in a three minute consultation?

"How long have you had this problem?" the doctor asked.\

"What problem?"

"You just told me that you were gay!" he snapped.

"I am, but it's not a problem."

He didn't ask any more questions. He wrote something on my papers and said, "That will be all. You have an appointment at 11:00 o'clock on Monday to talk with the psychiatrist."

We all spilled out into Oakland Street, and I looked for the Quaker housewife but she had gone home, and now the flag waved proudly in the clouded sky. I bummed a ride back to San Francisco from the guy with a brown mustache and the serious poet's eyes. He said that he was going to come back to talk to the shrink also, because by accident the doctor had talked him into saying he had suicidal tendencies and now he was talking himself into it.

"Aren't you the guy with the black bathing suit?" he asked.

"Yes," I said apologetically, "but last week I had a beard and long hair."

"Oh, you're all dressed up."

"You got it. I was wondering how I looked. What did you think when you saw me? Did you think I was queer?"

"I thought that if you weren't, you deserved to get out anyway, just for having enough guts to go through the physical looking the way you did."

"I sure earned it." I shook my head. It was about supper time when he let me off in the city, and I was emotionally exhausted from having to deal with what seemed like an entire army of hostile vibes.

*****

In order to get my head straight, I knew I had to pile some positive vibes into it. I called Tieco, a tiny, beautiful Japanese girl, and asked her if she wanted to go hear Roland Kirk at the Fillmore Auditorium, and she said, "Sure." In a half an hour we were dancing under strobes and blacklights to the Electric Flag and Mike Bloomfield, who used to be with the Butterfield Blues Band.

When the set finished, we got seats near the front so that we could play closer attention to what was coming next. Much of the beauty in Roland Kirk is in the subtle things that tell the kind of man he is.

The group began to take the stage. Kirk came out onto the bandstand, sliding one foot before the other. He wore dark glasses and no one led him. Those who did not know that he was blind could not have guessed it from his movements on stage. He had several neck straps for horns hanging around his neck, and a kazoo, and what I later found out was a siren attached to him near the neck so that he could reach around and utilize any of these other sounds in his music.

He played several tight jazz arrangements, and in the middle of a lick, when the jazz violin and the bass were going at it hard, he reached around his neck and started a low, and then an increasingly louder siren wail into the microphone, and the other instruments droned their sounds to meet the intensity of the siren, and the song took off.

Kirk did a standard called, "Baby Don't You Go." After a while he waved his hand from the audience toward the bandstand. He waited, and waved his arm, and soon several people echoed him: "Baby Don't You Go." The instruments set the scene, and Kirk sang on with his audience, a huge echo of hundreds of voices.

The next tune was an uptempo thing that began with the sound of three saxophones in harmony. Kirk held all three mouthpieces in his mouth at the same time. The tune began in the lower range of the baritone sax, ran up and down the scales of three horns, and then up as high as the limitations of the horn would allow. The second horn took over without any pause in beat, rhythm, or expression, so that it sounded as if he played only one instrument. Up to the small soprano sax, and then back to the lower. Up through the middle and all around every octave of all three horns, sometimes two at once, in harmony. A lower horn note was held, an upper horn worked in melody lines, and after the musicians traded licks for a while, Kirk ran up the entire range of all three horns. He grabbed hold of the kazoo and let out a wheeeeeeeeeee, and reached into the mouth of the biggest sax with his free hand and, snatching out his gold flute. He ran the scale up into the pure sweet sounds of the flute in clear upper octaves. There was nowhere else to go. The audience went wild. We were all screaming at the top of our voices when the siren began to wail, and I thought the walls would come down. It was hard to believe that there was something else to be said musically after that, but

Roland Kirk did his final number with the audience invited in. The tune was quite long. When each musician finished trading licks, and the song was working, Kirk shuffled toward the edge of the stage. He made his way slowly, stepping down in front of the bandstand without stumbling. He walked back and forth in front of the lights, still playing the tune, bumping into the lights, sending the stage lighting soaring into the air, arcing around the huge room. Kirk climbed out onto the floor and walked among the crowd, still playing the song. Somehow a single piece of music stretched out into the audience. People made room for him, giving way. When he was in the middle of us, he played with one hand and pulled a package out of his back pocket with the other. He held it out for the audience, and thirty of us went and took little wooden flutes from his hand. A few of us made little exploratory toots, which Kirk heard, and the exact notes of which he echoed, half note or squawk, his other hand still playing the sax. When he had given out all the free flutes, he waved us into the music, shouting, "ALL RIGHT!"

You could here the wooden flute sounds coming from every part of the Fillmore Auditorium. The music moved faster and faster. Kirk began to walk slowly back, in rhythm to the stage, playing furiously, all the tiny flute sounds around him. He and we were surrounded by music and somehow it was one piece of sound, one song, and the crowds parted before him and filed in behind him, smiling and dancing and playing the magic flutes. We were a part of that which Roland Kirk believes to be one of life's most important things.

Kirk made his shuffling way, still playing, still without assistance and without missing a beat, back to the bandstand. The wooden flutes fell silent as if by common feeling. The musicians brought the tune to a tight ending, to clapping and shouting and joy. In the midst of the applause Roland Kirk took something else from his pocket, tore it in half, and threw it at the audience. Then he turned his back, groping around, gathered up his horns and his musicians, and left the stage. We were all still clapping wildly. I ran up onto the stage and came back with half of a dollar bill.

As I made my way toward my seat, several people asked me what it was. I tore it in half and gave parts of the torn buck to them, again and again. When I got back to Tieco, the piece I had left was no larger than a dime. I gave Tieco half, and she rolled it into a thin green line and made it part of the jade necklace she was wearing. We sat still for a beautiful long while.

After the Kirk experience, the weekend was mild and relaxing. I told Lynn and Frank about what had happened over in Oakland. They laughed about the boots and the bathing suit. Then it was Monday and I dressed up again for the meeting with the United States Army psychiatrist.

There was the waiting again. I sat next to a thin, muscular man who was a ballet dancer. It turned out that he was married but still did not have to complete the physical because he had told them he still had a male lover. He went in for the final interview.

My turn came. I went in and sat down, made a few nervous gestures with my hands. The doctor's sandy hair fell in his face, and he looked harassed and tired, but most terrifically bored. I'm sure he had never volunteered, but had been drafted into service. He read my papers and looked at my letter. I said, "Pardon me, but before we begin, could I ask a question.?"

"Sure," he said. "Go ahead."

"I've heard that these interviews are held confidential, but I may want to get a teaching job with the state, and if the records are accessible--"

"Come off it!" the doctor interrupted. "You admitted that you are a homosexual in your forms. You even have a letter from a private physician to that effect. And now you're worried?"

"My doctor's files are completely confidential," I said. "But I was wondering if any of the information that I give you would hurt me later on."

"You have nothing to worry about," he said. "Are you undergoing therapy now?"

"No, doctor."

"Do you expect to in the near future?"

"What for?" I was all innocence.

He did not answer. He wrote on the form, signed it, and gave it back to me. "That will be all," he said. He did not look at me.

It was all over without me having to say one dirty word to them. I felt as if I was floating. The Vietnam draft had hung over me for six years, and the fear and anxiety suddenly lifted.

After finishing a BA in creative writing at San Francisco state, I bummed around the Bay area for a year or so before John Gardner, my writing coach, asked me if I wanted to write or teach. If I wanted to teach, I should get a masters, and if I wanted to write I had the chance to live on his small farm in Southern Illinois and help him with his kids, feed the dogs, and train the horses. Off to the geographical heart of the country I drove in my VW van packed full of books and ideals. I stayed on Gardner's farm for two years, learning all the while. Then I found a place of my own with a stream for an eastern border. Little Indian Creek. Not far from Boskydell.

Made in the USA
Charleston, SC
10 October 2013